BY LAURIE NOTARO

Housebroken

The Potty Mouth at the Table

It Looked Different on the Model

Spooky Little Girl

The Idiot Girl and the Flaming Tantrum of Death

There's a (Slight) Chance I Might Be Going to Hell

An Idiot Girl's Christmas

We Thought You Would Be Prettier

I Love Everybody (and Other Atrocious Lies)

Autobiography of a Fat Bride

The Idiot Girl's Action-Adventure Club

HOUSEBROKEN

HOUSE-BROKEN

Admissions of an Untidy Life

LAURIE NOTARO

BALLANTINE BOOKS

NEW YORK

Published in the United States by Ballantine Books,
an imprint of Random House,
a division of Penguin Random House LLC, New York.

BALLANTINE and the HOUSE colophon are
registered trademarks of Penguin Random House LLC.

LIBRARY OF CONGRESS CATALOGING-IN-PUBLICATION DATA
NAMES: Notaro, Laurie, author.
TITLE: Housebroken : admissions of an untidy life / Laurie Notaro.
DESCRIPTION: New York : Ballantine Books, 2016.
IDENTIFIERS: LCCN 2016008624 (print) | LCCN 2016016990 (ebook) |
ISBN 9781101886083 (paperback) | ISBN 9781101886090 (ebook) |
SUBJECTS: LCSH: Notaro, Laurie. | Humorists, American—20th century—
Biography. | Women—Humor. | BISAC: HUMOR / Form / Essays. |
BIOGRAPHY & AUTOBIOGRAPHY / Personal Memoirs.
CLASSIFICATION: LCC PS3614.O785 Z466 2016 (print) |
LCC PS3614.O785(ebook) | DDC 814'.6—dc23
LC record available at https://lccn.loc.gov/2016008624

Printed in the United States of America on acid-free paper

randomhousebooks.com

246897531

Book design by Barbara M. Bachman

To Pam, Libby, and Jenny

CONTENTS

HOUSEBROKEN

BIRTH OF A HOARDER

My sister Lisa spent most of her early childhood in a Dumpster. Lifting her in, my Pop Pop would point to where she should root around like a little beaver with her hands, searching for stuff that drugstores deemed too unworthy to stock on their shelves anymore. Once, she found a comb still in its packaging and held it up like a prize, much to my Pop Pop's delight as he cheered and clapped for a job well done. On another hallowed day, she emerged from a mess of cardboard and trash with a clock radio in her hands and presented it to my grandfather, who reacted as if she had discovered a roll of gold Krugerrands.

"It's *in one piece*!" he shrieked with delight.

Convinced by her eight-year-old logic that if she found a packaged comb in the trash she certainly might find a Barbie in the same condition, my Pop Pop continued to dip my sister into Dumpsters until she gained enough weight that he sprained his back lifting her out. Mostly, their haul consisted of old bakery items and dented boxes of generic cornflakes, but their more resplendent heists often became decorations in his backyard, like a clown head he balanced on a stick in his garden to scare birds away from his tomatoes, and Mr. Arizona, a life-sized stuffed man doll with a mustache and top hat so terrifyingly shuddersome that even a pedophile wouldn't have touched him. Mr. Arizona sat on the back patio in his favorite chair, his long, ghoulish, stained legs stretched out like those of a plantation master, and as the neighborhood slipped into decline, he was, I am positive, the only reason my grandparents never got robbed. Tweakers like stealing, it is true, but even they are scared of dolls that could easily suck out your soul and an eyeball or two in the process. There is no doubt in my mind that there were the bones of at least three children still being marinated in Mr. Arizona's digestive tract, and when my grandfather died, Mr. Arizona found himself in the hands of Nana and heading toward the alley the minute we got home from the funeral.

Pop Pop was an avid collector of anything cheap and free, and if that meant lowering his tiny granddaughter into a stinking bin of trash and risking cholera to find a clock radio that never worked, then so be it. He used all the tools at hand. Nana never let him bring any of his findings into the house, insisting, "All of that junk has bugs in it!" so he had no other choice than to display his ongoing, curated collection in the backyard or, for the finer items, in his shed.

To my grandfather, everything had value. Everything could be used again. He was a product of the Depression, and nothing should ever be thrown away. Tinfoil was cleaned and flattened. Sandwich baggies were washed out. He saved dishes and plastic containers from frozen dinners. My sister's old dollhouse was perched in a tree where all the birds that got the crap scared out of them by the clown head went to shit. Then he retired and became a janitor for a middle school where he had an all-access pass to garbage, and his Lincoln came home stuffed every day with old books, chewed-on pencils, and tossed art projects. Do you know how bad a middle school art project has to be before an art teacher will throw it away? In seventh grade, my left-brained nephew made a clay bowl with two scoops of ice cream and a banana resting in between them, and glazed it all the same color. Vanilla. It was supposed to be a banana sundae, but it was not a banana sundae. It looked like something you would pay for in a back alley in Thailand. *My sister still has it.* It's in a closet and she charges admission to see it, but *she still has it.*

That's how bad middle school art projects are that get tossed. Pop Pop had a collection of sculptures and masks that was nothing short of children's nightmares. Some of the masks had teeth, which is stark terror in and of itself, and several of the bust sculptures resembled burn victims, glazed in a delicate pink. Nevertheless, my grandfather placed these about his yard, hanging the masks on the cut fronds of a fat date palm that he paid to have decapitated because it produced too much messy fruit that Nana insisted was attracting bugs. It became a squat, thick altar of horror that he thought was "cute," and he continued to add elements to it until it contained pinwheels, ribbons, and totem poles that he found on clearance at Walgreens.

I'm sure his neighbors believed that the nutjob next door was practicing voodoo instead of being a little old Italian man who had nothing to do in baseball's off-season; all that was missing from his creation were chicken bones and a black candle. While I won't turn Elizabeth Gilbert on you and claim that he saw beauty in everything, he saw *use* in everything, even a green-glazed mask that I think was supposed to be the Hulk but more closely resembled the symptoms of the plague.

And this, along with toenails so thick I could roof a house with the clippings, is what I inherited from Pop Pop. Who was the girl who spent her lunch hours roaming thrift stores to furnish her first apartment? Me. Who was the girl who continued to shop at thrift stores on her lunch hour even when the apartment had everything? Me. Who is the girl who still buys a vintage dresser for ten dollars even if she has four others in the basement and a husband who has started to make her haul this stuff home by herself? The same girl who already has in her basement two complete bedroom sets, a couch that she will someday reupholster, a desk that will someday squeeze into the house, three antique doors that will fit into a house eventually, a lead glass window six feet tall and four feet wide that was salvaged from a neighboring house, and a stove.

But I am not a hoarder. I can give things away. I once traded a Victorian couch and a cast-iron sink to my farmer friends for a year's worth of polenta and beans. Which I also still have, but that is beside the point. I can throw things away, like credit card bills I have not paid. I even had a garage sale this past summer, which proves beyond a doubt that I am not a hoarder.

Before my beloved next-door neighbor Freddie moved, we decided to have a block sale to increase traffic and hopefully get rid of all of our unwanted stuff. The week before, I went through cupboards, closets, and the basement to collect enough items for a fairly good showing, if only to prove to my husband that I could part with things even if I felt they still retained a good use.

But I surprised even myself.

Seriously, if a museum had a garage sale, mine would have rivaled it, and if I could have named it, it would have been called "The Most Super Awesome Yard Sale EVER." I had antiques, hardcover books, clothes from Anthropologie from when I was still an Anthropologie size, incredible framed art, stoneware bowls, a telescope, and even a "FREE" box with old vases and jars.

"Why don't you save yourself a day and take all of this straight to Goodwill?" my husband said, and I stopped dead in my tracks.

"Are you kidding me?" I stormed. "Do you know how much this stuff is worth? I could make a thousand dollars tomorrow! This is gold, and I am basically giving it away. No way. I'm going to make a fortune tomorrow. Freddie put her sale on Craigslist. I'm just going to sit there and take money all day long."

"Do I have to help?" he asked.

"If I get an unmanageable crowd fighting over things, yes," I told him. "But you can wait until you hear me screaming for you."

I washed and lint-rolled all of the clothes. I folded them carefully and put them in bins. I lined up all the books, organized by the color of their spines. I set up a little table with a very pretty tablecloth to signify that this was The Most Super Awesome Yard Sale EVER and a chair, and I waited for the crowds to descend. My yard was full of treasures that my husband had been terrorizing me to donate to a thrift store, but all this stuff was worth something. The Arts and Crafts chalk sketches of fruit were still in their original tiger-oak frames. The antique steamer trunk retained Victorian lining paper inside. The telescope had been used once before my husband decided that astronomy was confusing and he needed a simpler hobby that didn't require calculations. The stoneware bowls were brand-new and priced at seventy dollars apiece on the potter's website. The Kenneth Cole suitcases would never be used again unless we went on a norovirus cruise and required vast amounts of Imodium A-D and Gatorade.

And then, the crowds did descend.

On Freddie's house.

As I waited for the overflow, my first customer wandered into my yard and went absolutely nuts in the clothing bin (as I told my husband people would), and draped skirts, pants, and shirts over her arm.

"I want all of this!" she said excitedly and then cooed over the fabric I had put out in another bin. "I'll take this one. And this one. And this one. You have such good taste!"

I smiled bashfully.

"What's this?" she said, picking up a VHS copy of *Out of Africa*. "*I love this movie!* Sold!"

"Wonderful!" I said, making a tally. "That's . . . forty-two dollars. How 'bout I throw in the movie for free? So that would be forty-one."

"It's a deal!" the lady said. "I'm Alyssa's mom, she lives across the street. She's over at Freddie's right now and has my purse, so I'll come back and pay you in a minute. Can I just leave the stuff here?"

"Absolutely," I agreed.

She flitted back over to Freddie's as another customer wandered over to the Arts and Crafts chalk sketches and picked one up by the top of the frame, which stayed in his hand as the rest of the frame and sketch remained on the grass.

My mouth fell open as he walked toward me and was about to hand over the thirteen dollars he owed me for destroying an original piece of antique art.

"Um, here," he said as he handed me the piece of tiger oak instead, and then found the "FREE" box.

"Is this really free?" he asked, this time holding up the entire vase that had come with some flowers I had gotten years ago.

"Sure is!" I said cheerfully, ready to accept his payment

as he hugged the vase and then walked away, but not before he looked at the Kenneth Cole luggage, wiped some spiderwebs off of it, and then moved on.

Then Spiderweb Guy rolled in on his black bicycle, a man I had seen around town several times since we moved to Eugene. Always dressing in layers of black, he wears black combat boots, a black bandanna around his head, and a black crocheted spiderweb over half his face. Judging by the scent cloud that trails behind him, I believe he smokes a considerable amount and is not concerned with secondhand stench. I held my breath as he came closer to my table and change center, bracing myself for the unexpected, because it takes one kind of nut to look at a crocheted black spiderweb and think it is cool, so add a couple extra layers of nut butter on top of that for the one who uses it as a tablecloth across his face for a "signature look."

I already knew there was nothing in The Most Super Awesome Yard Sale EVER for Spiderweb Guy, but I wasn't about to tell him that lest he decide to take it out on my merchandise and kick a whole bin of cassette tapes to death. Seriously. I had a still-in-cellophane Crowded House tape along with the first Big Country album that I bought twice, as a precautionary measure in case the first tape ever wore out. But he continued to sniff through all of my stuff, past the box set of *Sex and the City* DVDs, past a rather thick and wavy coffee-table book about beauty pageants that I spilled a Snapple on, and simply refused to consider my art collection as he dragged his black bike all over my yard.

Then he held up a vase and mumbled "Free?" to which

I nodded, so he put it under his arm and rode away with it. I have never felt so guilty letting a vase go to such an uncertain fate in all of my life. I suppose I should just be glad it didn't have legs so it couldn't be trafficked and forced to dance for a dollar behind glass for fat old men somewhere in Florida.

One old lady pulled up and offered me a quarter for a microwave cookbook I got for my wedding and had marked fifty cents, and I recalled my friend Amy's story about how she lost her shit at her last garage sale. After a day trying to unload her stuff onto strangers in the blazing Phoenix sun, one man told her she was asking too much for a fifty-cent dish and offered her a quarter for it. She looked him in the eye and said, "No. It's fifty cents," then snatched it out of his hand and sat on it, declaring, "Now I'm giving it to Goodwill. Find it there and pay two dollars for it."

But instead, I said, "Just take it," because I was too tired to do the math and give her change.

When my other neighbor came over and looked at the telescope, I told her the same thing, and she hauled the box home but came back in ten minutes to ask if I knew where the telescope stand was.

I shrugged. "In Phoenix?" I guessed, and suggested that maybe she could balance the three-foot-long item on the back of a chair or on one of her kids' shoulders as they took turns looking through it.

And that was it. Except for a cute group of college-aged kids that parked in front of my house and browsed through the books and DVDs.

"Is this *Sex and the City*?" one very cute girl asked me. "I can't read it through the dust."

"Take it," I said.

"I love this book on beauty pageants," one guy said. "But do all of the pages stick together?"

"It's been Snappled," I said. "But you can take it. Free."

They smiled nicely and said, "We like your books."

"Take all of them," I offered, but they looked at me oddly.

"We mean the ones you write," one of the cute girls said.

Oh shit.

"We saw your Facebook post," the other one offered.

"Oh," I said, remembering my post about The Most Super Awesome Yard Sale EVER because I am an asshole and didn't think anyone could find my house. "You should have been here an hour ago. That's when the good stuff was still here."

"Yeah," they nodded. "Looks like you've been cleaned out of the good stuff."

"Yup," I nodded. "Just odds and ends left."

"Would you sign these?" one of the girls said, producing *Idiot Girls* from her purse, and the other pulling *Spooky Little Girl* from hers.

And just like that, it really did become The Most Super Awesome Yard Sale EVER, and I made a note of emphasizing in the inscriptions that not all of my stuff was as dirty as what they saw on the lawn.

I was packing up after they left when my husband came out and asked me what I was doing.

"I'm throwing in the towel," I said, then showed him my wad of cash. "But I made thirty dollars."

"Twenty-five of that is my change," he informed me.

"Once the lady across the street pays me, I'll have made forty-five dollars," I corrected.

"Wait a minute," my husband said. "You offered a lay-away plan? She's never going to pay you."

"Her daughter lives right across the street; of course she's going to pay me," I said. "Have some faith!"

Then I picked up the box she had put all of her stuff in and walked it across to Alyssa's house.

There was no one home, but I left it by the front door.

When I returned, my husband stood in the front yard and asked me what my plan was. Essentially, it was to vacate the premises before any of my neighbors started bringing things back.

"Put it all in the car," I sighed, then saw he already had half of The Most Super Awesome Yard Sale EVER in there.

He made me drive to Goodwill because he said he wanted no responsible part in the surrender that I could blame him for later.

So it is true. I drove up to the donation area of the thrift store, and two employees came forward to help me. With the price tags still on them, I handed over the remains of the day. I felt Pop Pop looking down at me, shaking his head. "All of that is so cute," I could hear him say. "You have a whole backyard to put that stuff in!"

I got the receipt from one of the Goodwill guys and as I turned, I spotted a Chippendale leg poking out from underneath a pile of stuff that someone else had just dropped off.

"Oh my god," I said quickly, and pointed. "What is that?"

"Get in the car," my husband demanded and gave me a look that said he had no problem leaving me there.

I obliged, and started to pull away when I stopped and rolled down the window.

"One last thing," I said, and then handed the Goodwill guy a broken piece of tiger-oak framing.

Two weeks later, Alyssa's house was empty. She'd moved, along with my stuff from the garage sale. Apparently, I wasn't offering a layaway plan after all.

But I am sure, if I look hard enough, I will find my An-thropologie clothes, an *Out of Africa* VHS tape, and some familiar fabric at a Goodwill store, eventually.

THANK YOU FOR
BEING UNFRIEND

I guess I knew it was coming. I just couldn't believe it had actually happened.

I was speechless.

Months ago I giggled with my sister when she called me and said, "Guess what? Dad's on Facebook!"

It *was* funny. My father, one of the smartest guys I know, still hadn't quite gotten the hang of email, and filed his most important ones in his Trash folder so he "knew exactly where they were" because he didn't realize you could create a folder called "Important Emails I Should Not Keep in the Trash."

"He asked me to help him set up his profile," she said. "So now every time he logs on, he calls me to ask what his password is. But I'm not supposed to tell anyone he's on Facebook. He says he wants to take it slow."

"I agree that process is best," I said. "So please don't tell me his profile picture has an obscene amount of cleavage in it."

My sister paused. "Well," she said slowly. "I suppose

you could call it man-cleavage. He's sitting on his favorite Porsche."

"Not the re—" I started.

"Yes, the red one," she replied.

I winced.

I suppose Facebook was the next logical step after my father retired. He spent forty years building a construction-engineering business and had reached the top of his game, and was known as an expert in his field. When he finally decided to take it easy, the man who spent a hundred hours a week working had a lot of time on his hands.

So he joined the local YMCA and started lifting weights and bringing home stories of the new friends he made there.

"Such a nice bunch of young guys," he commented. "They come every day. I started talking to a couple of them, and they're so friendly. They call me Sarge."

"They call you what?" I asked.

"Sarge," he replied a little proudly. "I wear my ARMY T-shirt."

"But you were never a sergeant when you were in the Army, Dad," I replied.

"I parachuted out of a plane," my father shot back. "I earned it!"

"The Army didn't see it that way, Private," I replied. "But if your little friends want to give you a promotion, that's fine."

"They are nice guys, but some of them disappear and new ones pop up," my father continued. "But they all come together and leave together. One day I was leaving at the same time, so we all walked out to the parking lot.

I figured they all worked together, so I told them to have fun back at the office."

I nodded.

"And then they said they weren't going back to work," my dad said with a shrug. "They said they were all going back to rehab."

I was quiet for a second.

"You mean," I said with a crinkled brow, "you made friends with the halfway house guys?"

"They're nice guys," he said. "Some of them are scruffy, one of them smells, but overall, you know, nice guys."

"When they call you Sarge again," I added, "ask them how they knew you were a cop, just in case they try to ensnare you into being part of their crew."

So apparently, along with making friends with parolees, my father also wanted to broaden his social media view, possibly to connect with people on probation or those currently under indictment.

When I got his friend request, I did what everyone does: moan a little, think, *Well, that's the last time I can use the f-word on here,* and, finally, hit "Confirm." After all, what are you going to do? This is the man who took me to ballet lessons every Saturday, fed and clothed me for twenty years until I moved out, bought me a car, paid for my wedding. I'm going to say no to being his Internet friend?

I clicked my acceptance, and we were Facebook Friends. I imagined us "liking" each other's posts, saying funny things about my mom on IM, and tagging each other on posts about inside jokes we had created when we started our own two-person FB group.

Instead, I got a phone call.

"Laurie," he said. "This is Daddy. Could you take down that thing you wrote about me and the guys at the gym? I don't think that's very funny about them comparing ankle bracelets in the locker room. They spot me sometimes, you know."

I took it down.

"Laurie," another phone call started. "This is Daddy. So what you said on the Internet about me not being a real Sarge? Some people from the gym might see that and start asking questions."

I took it down.

"Laurie," began another request. "This is Daddy. Listen. I am going on that Zumba cruise with the people from the gym, but I haven't decided on a roommate yet, and frankly, I don't want it getting out. You're going to start a fight between Frank and Bob, and honestly, I don't need that kind of drama in my life."

I took it down.

The next phone call was from my sister.

"Um," she began. "I don't know how to tell you this, but Dad asked me how he could eliminate you."

"What?" I gasped. "Disinherit me? He can't! I have six hundred dollars in my 401(k). I was planning on his dying for my retirement!"

"Me, too," she agreed. "But not disinherit . . . exactly. He . . . he . . . he doesn't want to be your friend anymore."

"Oh my god, I told him I would pay for my own dinner next time!" I said in a huff.

"No, not in real life," my sister clarified. "On Facebook."

"What?!" I asked incredulously. "I took down every-thing he asked me to! And that stuff was gold, too. A-plus material. Did you know he's going on a Zumba cruise?"

"Yes," my sister said. "But now Bob is not speaking to him because of Frank."

"He's also taking spinning," I added. "And I haven't even touched that yet. Or the yoga."

"I know," she said. "Mom said it's not very manly."

"I could mine that for six jokes, easy," I scoffed.

"I know," my sister said sympathetically.

"Easy," I emphasized. "So what did you say? Am I being eliminated?"

"Nah," my sister said. "Dad doesn't even know his pass-word. I told him unfriending isn't allowed. He'll never fig-ure it out."

"I don't understand why he wants to *unfriend* me," I said, exasperated.

"He said you post too many pictures of your dog and your food," she explained. "He said he already knows what your dog looks like, and the photos of meals you had already eaten were disgusting. Like looking at a carcass."

"Those were ironic," I said, almost shouting. "I'm an anti-foodie! It's *supposed* to be gross. Get it? Get it? *How can you not get it?*"

"He didn't get it," my sister said. "Just leave a nice mes-sage on his wall tomorrow. It's his birthday."

"I already sent him a case of Devil Dogs," I complained. "The shipping alone was ten dollars."

"Then I can't help you," my sister answered, giving up.

"I thought I was his favorite," I said sadly.

"Oh, god no!" my sister replied, and burst out laughing. "I am!"

The next day, I realized she was right. I needed to buck up and, despite my anger about being almost eliminated, post a happy birthday message on my dad's wall. So I went to his page, and started to leave a message, but realized that I couldn't post. Or comment. Or "like." I couldn't do anything.

I was a ghost, clicking into thin air. He had unfriended me.

I will say that again. *My father unfriended me.*

MY FATHER UNFRIENDED ME.

What was I thinking? The man has built a courthouse, an airport, and most of Arizona State University. *Of course* he could figure out how to unfriend me!

I was so stunned at the action that it took more booze than usual to go to sleep that night. Sure, I unfriend people all the time; you have to curate your friend list sometimes, and toss the assholes, snarkers, and trolls. But eliminating me for no reason? That was just bad manners.

My therapist didn't even know what to say.

"Because of your dog and a picture of the last bite of a chili dog?" she asked. "Even though that sounds gross."

"It's *ironic*," I stressed again.

"Well, how does that make you feel?" she asked me.

"Hungry," I admitted.

"No, I mean your father discarding you," she explained.

"It makes me feel like posting that he is eating dark

chocolate and almonds in hopes of outliving my mother,"
I said. "And tagging her on it."

"Is that a good solution?" she asked.

"No," I replied. "But what if I put it up for a second and
took it down? I do that when I'm mad at my husband
sometimes. I don't know how many times I have to say, 'I
cook dinner. You clean up,' and then he leaves it all in the
kitchen and I'm stuck cooking and cleaning. So I wrote on
Facebook that from now on, I am charging him the market rate for every meal plus twenty percent gratuity if he
thinks he's living in a goddamned hotel. So I wrote that,
and posted it, and then I got an IM and forgot that I
posted it. And called him a shitface. His mom saw it."

"Remember when we talked about adding flour to the
fire as opposed to jet fuel?" she asked nicely.

"My dad *unfriended* me," I stressed. "It's like taking
me to an orphanage at the age of fifty. And I have to drive
because he can't see at night. In front of everyone I know!"

I stood on the sidelines when my sister posted that she
was taking a short break on a bench during an early morning jog and my dad commented, "That's my girl!" (My
comment: "Oh, look. Dad hasn't unfriended you yet.") I
watched as my sister posted pictures of her and my dad at
Easter and he "liked" them. (My comment: "I feel I have
to mention this again. My dad, same as Lisa's dad, UN-
FRIENDED me.") And a picture of her getting an award
at work. (My comment: "Remember when Dad unfriended
me?")

There was no resolution, and even though we never

really talked about it, the unfriending sat between us like a fart no one claimed. I just learned to live with it.

And as I was finishing this piece, writing the words "My dad unfriended me," a chime went off on my computer that I recognized as a Facebook chime. A distraction!!

There was a friend request pending; actually, there were three. One was a "mutual friend" with my friend Cecelia; another was a friend of my friend Melanie. And in the third profile picture was a guy sitting on top of a red Porsche with a lot of man-cleavage.

HOUSEBROKEN

*I*f there is one thing you ever need to know about me, it's that I once made raisins in my office by accident. And that they tasted *good*.

I never have been, and never will be, a tidy person.

And I'm not sorry.

First of all, I hate the word. Tidy. TIDY.

I'd much prefer "straighten," "clean up," and "organize" to "tidy."

Let me tell you about Tidy. She's smug, self-important, and frankly, just an asshole. Tidy wears her underwear too tight and has a lisp. Tidy looks down on everyone around her. Tidy is a vegan and that will be the first thing you know about her. She wears sweater sets and won't get a dog because she's afraid of it shedding. On her.

Tidy also makes more money than I do, has never cringed when her boss asks her to drive him to lunch because he read somewhere that it's something managers should do to undermine their employees, and has never lost grapes in her office.

I've never been her.

I was already a wreck by the third grade when my mother told me to clean my room until I could see the carpet. I did, and shoveled everything into the closet. The next day, when I came home from school and opened the closet doors, everything was gone. My mother had dragged it all to the trash can in the alley.

And I mean everything.

The glue, wood, and tools for the pieces of the dollhouse I was building; the pens, paper, and paints I was using to create the illustrations I was making for my first book cover; my ice skates that I took the blades off of to resemble *Little House on the Prairie* boots that I would wear with a long gingham dress to make me really feel the part as I wrote a play about pioneers on the Oregon Trail; and all seven of the books I was reading at the same time. All of it, dumped.

I sobbed as I retrieved what I could from the garbage and said goodbye to what I couldn't reach.

When my mother saw me bleary-eyed and red-faced, clutching the ice skates to my chest, white-knuckled, she said simply, "Cleaning your room doesn't mean moving the mess from the floor into the closet. What if you had to hide in there if Nazis came to get you? Do you think Anne Frank was messy? Because I can tell you right now that *she was not.* She lived for two years in a closet! *And* wrote a book!"

But it didn't work. I never got any more organized, I never became any more well-kept or orderly.

I've spent a lot of time trying to figure out why my sisters are both very neat and I am not. My mother keeps a house more immaculate than a space station, and my Nana vacuumed every day, although I never once saw her vacuum cleaner.

You can make an unannounced stopover at any of their houses and it would be all right. They'd even let you in. They might feed you cake. But you're not coming into my house if you don't give me twenty-four hours' notice and make a reservation first. And you sure as shit aren't getting cake, because that isn't enough time for me to clean my kitchen and make it.

So I asked my mother why she thought I was messy when the rest of our family isn't.

"Well, I'll tell you, but you're not going to like it," she said. "Are you ready?"

"Yes," I replied.

"It's not because you're a creative genius," she informed me. "It's because you're lazy. You were neat as a little girl. You put your toys away."

"Like at what age?" I asked.

"Two," she said.

"I clearly had no outside interests then," I replied. "I don't see how that is a fair assessment. My days were pretty wide open when I was two. The only things I had to do were poop, eat, and sleep. Every two-year-old has time to clean up!"

So I asked my husband—who was a neat person when we got married, but has since been turned—the same question.

"I know you want me to say you're a creative genius,"

he said. "I can't tell you why you are messy, because I don't know. But maybe it's just better if I show you."

Then he got up, took two steps, looked at a piece of mail, started to open it, then saw the issue of *Vanity Fair* that had just been delivered, walked over to it as the letter fluttered to the floor, opened the magazine, then looked up, walked to the TV and changed the channel, then put on a hat that was next to the television, and then went upstairs, never to return.

I waited five minutes before I called out to him.

"I'M WORKING!" he screamed down at me.

"You're still doing the impression, aren't you?" I asked.

He came back downstairs and just shrugged, raising his eyebrows.

"You know, Einstein's office was a wreck, so was Mark Twain's, and Steve Jobs's was a disaster," I retorted.

"Well," my husband said. "Make me an iPad, then."

"So what is your answer?" I asked.

He sighed. "I think you're like a dog. You live in the moment, and when something looks attractive, you go toward it. When something bores you, you leave it for something more exciting, even if that means letting a pound of clay, thirty-two bottles of paint, and fourteen paintbrushes dry out because you needed to make strawberry jam."

"The strawberries were going to turn," I said in my defense. "It was now or never for them. The witch doll I was painting could wait. She wasn't going to grow mold. But then I went back and put all of my paintbrushes in water so they wouldn't dry out."

"And they are still at the kitchen sink in that cup a month later," he said.

"Yes, but I didn't let them dry out," I insisted.

"When are you going to clean them?" he asked.

"When I have time," I answered.

"You have time now," he said.

"No I don't," I said. "I have an eBay auction in three minutes for dollhouse windows and then I need to finish the collar for the dress I'm sewing."

"So maybe tomorrow?" he asked.

I winced. "I dunno. I have a piece to write for the new book, and then I have to make cheese. And I need to secretly place a copy of a story from *The New York Times* about how chickens attract rodents in our neighbor's mailbox without being seen. Tomorrow's kinda booked. Oh, yeah. And then I have to go to the thrift store to find a pot big enough to dye my green dress gray because I got bleach on it the last time you made me clean. Yeah. No way the brushes are going to happen tomorrow."

"What about the next day?" he asked.

I sighed. "I have a therapy appointment, then I have to make a diorama for my book cover. Get it? And I am going to have to hit every Safeway in town until I find one that has five cases of Canada Dry Ten because it's buy two get three free, and I am NOT mixing and matching with 7UP Ten because 7UP Ten completely sucks and I am never making *that* mistake again."

Then I posted a picture of my office on Facebook, and people freaked out. Yeah, it was a little messy, mainly because one of my stacks had fallen over onto the floor the week before last and made it look way worse than it was. People called me a hoarder and told me to "get your shit together."

"My shit IS all together," I commented back. "ON that table. That is exactly what I am showing you!"

And hoarders, by the way, make paths. If you don't have a path to get to your hoarder table, you are legally not a hoarder. You're a collector. And it was plain as day that I could walk up to the table and touch anything on it as long as I didn't mind stepping on a couple of books and some dishes, which was awesome, because I had been looking for them.

I have to say that I was surprised at most of the reactions and comments about the picture; I have written about the archeology of cleaning my room in one of the books, surprised at what I was finding, layer by layer; that I once discovered the remains of a dead woman in my scary room; and that I hands down beat the DEA when they attempted to search my house for drugs and actually gave up halfway through my closet. I wasn't making any of that stuff up. So how could people be so shocked when they saw a picture of the actual thing? Even my editor, who has gone over a majority of my writing with a fine-tooth comb, wrote back "Yikes!" when she saw the picture.

Did no one believe me besides my mom?

Maybe I am messier than the average messy person, I thought. Maybe my messiness is so awful that people tend to think I am exaggerating. Even my husband thought I was blowing the situation out of proportion when we began dating until, as he tells the story: "I went to put beer in your fridge and there weren't any shelves. Everything was in a big pile on the bottom, accented with bits of broken glass. You said to just put the beer on top. I had to talk myself out of fleeing immediately."

The good news is that while quite overstuffed, my fridge now has all of its shelves still intact, but the bad news is that if I was in my twenties again, making seventy bucks a week, and all of my refrigerator shelves broke one by one, I still wouldn't replace them.

Anyway, I got the Tidy book, the book that can make anyone Tidy and promises to be foolproof. Everyone who knows me has been telling me to get that book, so I stuck through it after the author professed that she started reading home and lifestyle magazines when she was five, though I did roll my eyes. When she asked the question, "Have you ever been unable to study for an exam the night before and found yourself tidying instead?" I shook my head, and a crumb from the chocolate muffin I was eating tumbled out of my mouth onto the floor when I answered, "No, I usually found myself *drunk* instead."

I pushed through the part where she claimed, "A messy room equals a messy mind," and sighed slightly. And when she stated, on page thirty-one, that "when it comes to being tidy, the majority of people are lazy," I laughed a little.

Further on, when she suggested that you ask each and every object if it sparks joy, I thought that I might finally have a good reason to dump my elliptical machine, but I did walk over to my craft table and clear my throat.

"Dress pattern from 1939 with the Peter Pan collar, inverted-V bodice, and poufy little sleeves, do you bring me joy?" I asked, holding it up, and then I giggled. "Of course you do! Especially when I make you up in that gray-plaid seersucker in the fabric closet right there, or the pale-pink silk on the silk shelf, or that wonderful floral voile that I got in New York. Of course you bring me joy! That was a silly question!"

It was such a waste of time that I didn't bother asking the other fifty-three patterns on the table the same thing.

"Empty Altoids box," I queried. "Do you bring me joy? Of course you will, once I make a little circus diorama in you with paper cutouts of flying girls and prancing horses! And then I'll make a little theater out of this empty Altoids box, and out of this one I'll make a little travel-sized sewing kit."

I moved on. "Random Styrofoam egg-shaped thing, do you bring me joy?" I asked, then paused. I was not sure.

"I'm going to bring you a shitload of joy when you realize you need me to make a spur-of-the-moment doll head and you're happy that you didn't purge me because you also purged the forty-percent-off coupon you got from Michaels yesterday. Idiot," the egg-shaped thing shrieked at me.

"By god, you're right!" I exclaimed. "You get to stay!"

Then I looked at all of the other things on my table. Vintage velvet ribbon. A thimble my friend Louise brought back from England when she went to the Alexander McQueen show. A dupioni purse I was halfway finished with. A scattering of antique jet buttons. An assortment of sculpted doll heads I hadn't painted yet. Scraps of the softest leather that waited patiently to be made into purses someday.

"AAAAAAAAAAAAAA!" I screamed, unable to keep it in. "I am bursting with joy! I love all of my things!"

Nevertheless, I continued on in the book, and got to the part where she undresses each night and thanks her clothes for making her productive and helping her accomplish a lot.

Um.

But I tried it. If it would help me hang up my dirty clothes, so be it. The first night I said to my shirt, "I'm sorry I got so fat I ripped your arm seam out. I'm sure that hurt."

The second day I said to my dress, "I'm sorry I peed a little in you today. But I'm at that age when we need to expect that from time to time."

And on the third day, I told my vintage green sweater, "I'm sorry the saag paneer didn't make it all the way to my mouth and dropped right on the boob portion of you. It will probably be a while before I try to get the stain out, but with a boldly placed brooch or if my hair grows six more inches, I'll probably wear you again."

Then the Tidy lady wrote how she was shocked when one client had an unbelievable eighty rolls of toilet paper in his house. I glanced sideways and said to myself, I am looking at that right now. No way I'm letting the apocalypse go down without at least eighty rolls of Charmin blue in my direct line of vision.

But when I got to the part where she talked about

throwing away books that hadn't been read, I had had enough and closed the book. Those words are nothing short of the rantings of a lunatic. Madness. Enough, I thought, *enough*. Tossing books you've never read is not just a sin, it's a crime, one worthy of capital punishment. Frankly, if I walk into your house and you *don't* have two hundred books somewhere that you haven't read yet, I don't trust you. I don't want to know you as a person. I barely believe you are human. But if you don't have the capacity to want, if you lack the urge to find out, if you're not curious enough to explore the stories you don't know yet, or what is in the book that you brought home for whatever reason, I have to say this is the point where I believe civilization stops, curls up in a ball, and dies a dull, boring, very tidy death.

And I want no part of it. Or your magically tidy house, which, by the way, I find lifeless, a shell, a corpse of something probably once vibrant and bursting with things to make, read, touch, feel, smell, and explore. She's a kook, I finally determined, and I suspected it all along. I had already read about her texting goodbye to an old phone when she got a newer model, and supposedly, the old phone got the text and subsequently died. She is a madwoman. If anyone told you that story while waiting in the checkout line at Safeway, would you change lanes? I would. You can kill someone with a Hershey bar or a copy of *The Star,* you know.

If someone told you at Thanksgiving dinner that they thanked their clothes before hanging them back up again at night (and I'm not even going to address the part about hanging up *dirty* clothes), would you trust them with the knife to cut the pumpkin pie? I don't even want to sit next to someone like that on the subway. I don't want to even sit in the stall next to them, a thin piece of tin barely separating me from a woman who thinks magic consists of sucking the soul out of a house.

I know why I am not tidy. It took reading that compact, perfect little book to find out. It's because I HATE it. To me, tidying every day is the equivalent of sitting down after dinner and figuring how much money you owe the IRS from the money you earned that day.

I clean my house the way I do my taxes: in crisis mode. I wait until there is no alternative, and then I do it in one grand sweeping motion. And I've come to the conclusion that there is absolutely nothing wrong with that. This is the way I'm wired; this is the way I work. After reading the Tidy book, I am actually a little proud of how I operate. I don't care that the author calls messy people lazy; I've written thirteen books under towers of bills, IRS notices, old catalogues, sales statements, and receipts and binders full of research. And I hope to write thirteen more.

When I really boil it down, when I really think about it, I have to wonder, when I'm dead and gone, what do I hope someone puts on my headstone—Laurie Notaro, Messy, but Literally Laughed Herself to Death and Wrote Some Funny Books, or Laurie Notaro, Kept a Really Clean House and Paid Her Bills on Time?

So, know this. I never want to be Tidy. Tidy is most likely an alcoholic, but not an awesome one. She's the lady who you see in Rite Aid buying the five-dollar bottles of

Chardonnay in a six-pack so that it doesn't stain her teeth, and the one that never laughs when she's drunk—only cries.

That's sad. And that is not the way I want to live my life, even if I can't find the corkscrew in one of the five drawers I try first before eventually locating it under a couch cushion. And have to pull all of the dog hair off of it and let that float to the floor before I use it.

And to the lady who wrote the book about Tidy, I know that you cried when you found slime on the bottom of your shampoo bottle one day in the shower instead of exclaiming, "Science is awesome!" and rinsing it off, but what makes me cry is that you will never know the joy of losing grapes in your office and making raisins, even by accident, and that the raisins you made taste really good.

But understand, if you'll excuse me, I have found one thing in my house that does not bring me joy—a perfect, neat little book that can never tell me how to be happy. With a big wave goodbye, I release you into the recycling bin.

There. That was magic.

KISSSSSSS ME

*S*eriously. Who doesn't want almost free food?

And not only was it almost free, it was delivered to me, the meals of my choosing.

I didn't have to stand in line at a food bank, I didn't have to plead my case to the local Department of Economic Security, and things on the menu included steak, fried chicken, and korma!

All I had to do was buy a Groupon, and I'd get a week of HelloFresh meals for thirty-nine dollars, and if that meant that I didn't have to go to Safeway for a week, count me in.

Any excuse not to enter that vortex of mayhem otherwise known as Safeway is one that I will adopt, so I bought the Groupon and immediately signed up. The next week, on Wednesday, UPS would deliver an enormous package with each meal brilliantly organized in its own box with hipster ingredients (the tiniest jars of Sir Kensington's mustard and ketchup, organic herbs in their own miniature clamshells, and spice mixes in adorable paper bags with cute labels) and instructions.

As I unpacked the contents, my husband picked up the recipes and started looking them over.

"Do you know what I think would be awesome?" he said after a moment.

I looked up and shrugged.

"If we cooked *together*," he said. "I think it might be fun, and we could increase our couple coordination that way."

"You want to be a team?" I asked reluctantly. "You want us to be more coordinated?"

"Yes," my husband answered. "Don't you think that would be fun?"

"No," I said blankly. "I do not. I already know how to cook, and you are a six-foot, two-inch man, and this is a very small kitchen. We have like three square feet here. And you take up four."

Aside from his André the Giant stature, my husband is a master at Man Cooking, which is just basically throwing together two or three ingredients within his field of vision and ingesting it before his brain can identify that he is swallowing things people won't even eat in Africa. For example, he lays claim to the fact that he invented "Salsa Spaghetti," which entails boiling some pasta and christening it with Taco Bell sauce. Another favorite is a sleeve of saltine crackers smashed in a glass of milk and stirred, otherwise known in the civilized world as "spackle," and once, for a special treat on his birthday, he asked me to make him toast with canned vegetable soup poured over it.

"We have very different cooking styles," I replied. "I

like to make things I enjoy eating, and you make things like you're living by the river and cooking in a can heated by a Bic lighter."

"Well, maybe if we could work on our partnership skills, we wouldn't have been such a—" he started, then suddenly stopped.

"Ooooooooh," I said, shaking my pointer finger. "I get it. I get it. This is all about the Kiss Kam, isn't it?"

My husband waited for a moment.

"I'm just saying that if we had better timing together, we would have been more in sync and maybe that wouldn't have happened," he finally said.

"I know you want to blame me for the Kiss Kam, but it was not my fault," I stated without question. "That was not my fault."

My husband opened his mouth.

"NOTMYFAULT," I said loudly, and pointed my finger at him.

We had been married twenty years, happily, enjoyably, and satisfactorily. We were proud of our accomplishment, we were pretty much good with our life and the choices we had made. We drank wine in the evenings, we made each other laugh on a daily basis, and sometimes to the point of urination, which I found particularly impressive until that same thing started happening when I was simply trying to get out of bed in the morning. In any case, things were good. We were married. We felt that we had married the right people. There were no regrets, there were no shadows of doubt.

Until the Kiss Kam.

We recently got season tickets to Eugene's farm league baseball team, mainly because my husband discovered he likes baseball and I have always liked the dollar hot dogs and the twelve-dollar nachos. He bought us both baseball caps with the team logo on them. It's a great reason to get out in the beautiful Oregon summer weather, the mascot is Bigfoot, and there's always a chance an asshole is going to get hit in the head with a baseball. So far, that has come very close to happening, and the asshole was me.

But apparently, there's a lot of downtime in baseball and, thus, the reason for audience participation during those recesses. The corporations need their time (there is a Taco Race sponsored by Taco Bell, and a cheeseburger building race by Carl's Jr.); then there's the ring toss, in which little kids get a chance to win a free ice cream, and a tug-of-war that is usually hilarious, with a fat kid and a skinny kid on each end of the rope.

And then there's the Kiss Kam, which scans the stands for unsuspecting victims, looking for people who look like couples—which is a very dangerous proposition if you ask me, rife with the potential for a lawsuit. The camera then stays on the couple until they kiss.

Usually, this is the cue for either one of us to get nachos, but before I could even reach down and grab my wallet, my husband gasped.

"What's wrong?" I asked.

"Kiss Kam," he hissed between closed teeth.

"I know," I said. "I'm going to get nachos now."

"Tooooooo late," he hissed again, and motioned his eyes toward the baseball field screen to see my largest nightmare come to life. There I was, reaching down in between my legs for my purse, my eyes wide as saucers and my husband frozen as if he had just had a stroke or Darth Vader had turned him into carbonite.

"Holy shit," I saw my mouth say.

"You're going to have to kiss me," my husband struggled to emit.

"Act like brother and sister," I hissed back, the camera still on us.

Apparently, patting someone's leg indicated a sibling relationship in my husband's family, because that's exactly what he did. The cameraperson who steadied his camera on us, however, saw that as a symbol of commitment and kept the lens exactly where it was.

"It's not working," my husband slurred. "You're going to have to kiss me."

"Oh god," I said.

"Kissssssss me," my husband insisted.

I was mortified. Despite my past, I am a bit of a Victorian who would really prefer to abstain from public displays of affection if at all possible. I felt my face get super hot, and I tried to figure out what to do.

"Kissssssss me," my husband hissed again.

The pressure was enormous. I felt like I was getting sucked into a black hole and as the seconds ticked away endlessly, my husband finally turned toward me and I had no choice.

In hindsight, I remember the incident frame by frame. The slow approach of my husband's face coming toward me, the furrowing of my brow, the implication of reluctance, his lips reaching out toward mine, my lips puckering up toward his, coming together, closer, closer, closer until—

BAM!

The brim of his baseball hat hit me in the forehead, and the brim of mine hit his, and thus, reaching for one another but solidly stuck four inches apart, our puckery lips tried to reach the other side but only moved like little fishes in a bowl.

And we stayed like that for moments, trapped in an accident of physics or something of that order that simple minds fueled by one-dollar hot dogs and twelve-dollar nachos cannot easily comprehend. Governments have fallen and people have died dramatic, notable deaths in less time. When my husband realized our blockage and finally took off his hat and we successfully made contact, two thousand spectators and several baseball players from Costa Rica had witnessed the gold standard in Kiss Kam failure, so horrible that people didn't even laugh and simply grew silent, probably believing that they had, indeed, just watched a brother and sister kiss.

I never got my nachos that day. We just left. We honestly had no choice. It was either that or wait for the Kiss Kam to return at any time, and we already both had developed cramps.

"That was worse than when I tried to run the mile in seventh grade, thought I was having a heart attack, and demanded that the even slower girls behind me go back for help, and they did," I said as we trudged to the car.

"I have never been so horrified in my life," my husband said.

"No, no, no," I pooh-poohed him. "What about the time a drop of my face lotion got on the seat of the toilet and you wanted to go to the emergency room because you thought it was going to burn a hole through your ass?"

"Yeah? Well your face lotion had salicylic acid, which sears off warts," he countered. "My whole left side was on fire. To this day, I know you're lying about there not being a scar on that side. Someday, someone will tell me the truth."

The wound of the Kiss Kam Katastrophe sat on our marriage for the rest of the day, my husband analyzing every second of the play to see how we could have averted such disaster.

"I just can't believe we failed the Kiss Kam," he said repeatedly, until I couldn't take it anymore.

"The fact that we collapsed in the face of a public challenge is not our fault!" I asserted. "It's the manufacturers of the baseball hats that are to blame. They need to be retractable, so that when an intern with the baseball team homes in on you like the Death Star, you have some recourse. We had no warning, we never had a chance. Plus, you weren't the one who had her head in between her legs while wearing a dress on a hundred-foot screen."

"No, but I was the man who couldn't figure out how to kiss his wife!" he replied, and suddenly turned toward me. "Kiss me!"

"Fine," I sighed, and obliged.

We each leaned in, and it took less than a second for us to halt four inches apart, exactly as we had before.

"Take the damn hat off!" I cried.

"No," my husband said emphatically. "We need to practice. We need to prove that we can do it."

So for the next ten minutes, we had to practice kissing with our hats on, from one side to the other, taking turns from every angle and every direction. Then he made us try a stop, turn, and kiss maneuver to use if we ever got caught on the Kiss Kam again to stun everyone who had watched our disaster.

While the wound eventually healed, the scar of doubt remained as puckered and red as our searching lips on that awful day.

So when this new opportunity presented itself in the box of HelloFresh dinners, my husband wanted—no, demanded—that we use it to prove our in-tandem couple skills.

"We do plenty of things in tandem," I complained. "We watch TV together, we go to the movies together, we eat dinner together every night."

"But we can't eat popcorn out of the same bowl," he mentioned. "And that is a tandem activity."

"That's because you hover," I said. "And your hand is the size of a baseball glove. In fact, I've never seen you put popcorn into your mouth. Your hand is always just there, right above the bowl like it was a Magic Eight Ball. If I wanted to go as you for Halloween, all I would need is a bowl of some salty snack and my hand just hanging over it."

"Then that's proof that we need to work on our couple coordination," he said. "Let's just try it and see how it goes. Let's make a deal that we will cook these three meals together, and if it's another failure in our relationship spectrum, then we'll stop. I won't bug you again. I promise."

"What do I get for my trouble if all I get is aggravation?" I said. "What's in it for me if it doesn't work?"

He thought for a minute.

"I give you my permission as your partner, in the future, to have an individual popcorn bowl," he said, luring me in. "All to yourself."

"Fine," I said, giving in.

"Let's make one tonight!" he said, and I agreed, if only to hurry up and get this thing over with.

At six o'clock, he pulled out the box that held the seared steak dinner and put it on the kitchen counter.

"You ready?" he asked.

"Yep," I answered.

"Okay," he said, holding the recipe card. "There are four elements to this dish. How about we split it half and half? There's couscous, roasted cauliflower, romesco sauce, and the steak. Which portions of the dish do you want?"

I thought I would be kind. A baby could make couscous if it didn't require boiling water, and chopping some cauliflower seemed easy enough. "I'll take the steak and the romesco sauce," I said.

He winced. "I would really like to give the romesco sauce a shot. It looks like it has an interesting taste profile, and there's a lot of chopping. I'd like to work on my knife skills," he said.

I shrugged and tried not to laugh. This is the man who, when I'm out of town, eats Fritos and beans mixed together as if it's a French delicacy. "Okay, then . . . I'll take the cauliflower?"

"Sure," he said, tossing me the head as he went over to the knife block. Here we go, I thought to myself. We're going to argue over the best knife. This should be awesome.

Knife fight ten seconds in.

But he passed over my favorite knife, dawdled over my second favorite, then went to the top of the knife block, pulled out a cleaver, and went back to the cutting board with it.

"Really?" I said when he pulled out the red pepper. "You're going to start with the *Friday the 13th* knife? Let's calm down, cowboy, and take a run with a paring knife first."

He shook his head. "I like this one. Feels solid."

"You know," I said slowly, "if you took the pepper out to the driveway and ran over it with the car, it's the same amount of overkill as your ax there."

"Worry about yourself," he cautioned. "I'm not concerning myself with your choice of knife."

"No problem," I said. "But when you realize you only have four fingers on one hand, use one of them to call 911. Because I'm worrying about myself, you know."

"Thanks," he said. "The oven needs to be preheated to four hundred degrees."

"I already did that," I replied.

He put his sickle down and walked over to the oven, next to where I was cutting the cauliflower with the right-sized knife. "You only got it to three seventy-five," he said, as he turned the knob an increment. "Wait. STOP. STOP cutting the cauliflower. STOP. Please."

I stared at him and waited for him to say, "Watch out for that wilted piece," or "Oh my god, there's a worm!" but, instead, he picked up the instruction card and read aloud, "Cut the cauliflower into bite-sized florets."

Then he looked up at me.

"Yeah?" I replied.

"I think maybe you're taking the easy way out," he said earnestly. "You're a half inch over bite-sized there. Shouldn't bite-sized mean I should be able to pop it in my mouth? I couldn't do that with most of those."

I just stared at him.

"That one, right there, like, who has a mouth that big? Like Steven Tyler could eat that bite, Mick Jagger, sure. But to anyone else with an average-sized mouth, you're just going to run into trouble there," he continued. "You're promising something you can't deliver."

I paused.

"Considering that I'm sharing this meal with the person who has the biggest mouth on the planet, I'm not too worried," I said, and started chopping the cauliflower into egg-sized chunks.

"I'm just following directions," my husband said, and went back to his red pepper slaughter.

"Yeah, well, the recipe didn't call for a sword, but that did not deter you at all," I replied.

"I am comfortable with my food preparation decisions," he said, turning away from me.

"As am I," I retorted, leaving half of the cauliflower head intact as I shoved it into the oven.

I had the cauliflower roasting and was seasoning the steak when my husband posed a question.

"What exactly is a pinch?" he asked. "Does it matter which fingers I use? Because if I pinch with my pinky and thumb, that is considerably less than pinching with my thumb and forefinger. The water for the couscous requires a pinch of salt, but is that just a rhetorical reference?"

I stopped seasoning the steak.

"Would you do me a favor?" I asked. "Would you run upstairs and get that piece of paper that says you have a Ph.D. on it? The one with the gold sticker? I want to make sure you didn't get it from the University of Phoenix or the place where you draw the turtle and pirate."

"That's so funny, because I don't see a pinch of sarcasm anywhere in the ingredient list," he said. "Careful it doesn't leave a bitter taste in your mouth and ruin the dish."

"How about I show you what a pinch feels like?" I asked.

He put down his scythe and turned toward me.

"I thought we were supposed to be a team doing this together," he said. "But when it comes down to the flavors and the execution, I am not taking the blame for your mistakes."

"Are you saying you'd throw me under the bus?" I asked.

My husband just shrugged. "I'm just saying I'm not going down because of your attitude."

I gasped.

"You have four minutes until my steak is done," I said harshly. "And then it's hands up. *Partner.*"

I tossed my steaks into the sizzling pan, crushed the garlic, removed the cauliflower from the oven, and drizzled it with olive oil and some Parmesan cheese that was *not in the recipe.* I was taking matters into my own hands, creating the profile I knew would work, and with thirty seconds left and counting, I flung the last tablespoon of butter into the pan and let the steaks rest in the foam as it sizzled.

"Who turned my burner off?" my husband screamed as he tended to his couscous. "My burner's off!"

". . . three, two, one," I said, slapping my steak tongs down on the kitchen counter. "Hands up!"

My husband sighed and put his hands up.

"I didn't get to plate," he said bitterly, shaking his head. "Sabotage."

"I didn't touch your burner," I said.

"Let's just eat," he suggested.

And, as we sat down at the coffee table where we eat because we are savages, my first bite of steak was awesome, and because I took all of the bite-sized pieces of cauliflower, our meal rocked. My husband's couscous, despite the irresponsible approach to salt, was delightful, with raisins and pistachios in it. The romesco sauce was the perfect pairing for the steak, and three bites in, we complimented ourselves on a job well done.

"I like the Parmesan," he said. "Worth the risk."

He turned his head from me, stopped, then he whipped it around, yelling "Kiss Kam!" and came at me, all puckered up.

I DO NOT WANT SHIT
IN MY SHOES

I unabashedly started to cry.

Maybe it was because our longtime mailman, Dave, had recently retired, maybe it was because my colorist had up and moved, or maybe it was that I had just found out that Trader Joe's had discontinued their grilled eggplant, but this was too much.

My adaption threshold had just been breached.

"But you can't move!" I insisted to my next-door neighbor Freddie, who looked at me with pleading eyes. "You're one of the only neighbors who hasn't called the cops on me!"

"We're getting older," she said to me patiently. "We just can't keep up with the maintenance of a big house anymore."

"I promise I'll start wearing pants when I walk around the side of my house that faces yours," I said. "I really will this time!"

"It's too late," my neighbor replied as she sighed. "We already found another home."

We had been neighbors for ten years, a solid ten years, a neighborly ten years, full of sharing holidays, eating dinner at one another's houses, and giving out sugar and curry powder when Freddie was in the middle of a recipe and realized she was short on ingredients. If I ran out of milk while making a cake, I'd just run next door, where she'd offer me soy milk and I'd make an exaggerated vomiting sound and say, *"No thanks!"*

Our houses were on a slight hill, and hers rose just above mine and we'd talk over our deck railings to each other on a daily basis, as if we were in a Lower East Side tenement. Being that my bedroom window was only a few feet away from her living room, on summer nights when we all had our windows open, I'd fall asleep listening to Freddie's television, reminding me of when we used to live with my grandparents in New York. It was a warm, comforting memory and made me feel like I was five years old again.

I loved having my friends live next door.

We shared hoboes. We shared squirrels. We even shared a raccoon couple until two years ago when they were both hit by a car while crossing the street.

I called 911 when Freddie's husband, Ed, fell off a twenty-foot ladder onto his back, and I was so scared I *ran* over to her yard when I heard him yell. I can prove it. There were witnesses. Ed recovered, but I still get a burn in my ankles that happens every time I walk faster than shopping speed.

I delivered the news to my husband that night, and he was equally bereft. "I am so sad to see them go, they were such good neighbors," he said. "I wonder what kind of neighbors we're going to get now."

I suddenly felt as if Freddie had shown me a carton of soy milk.

"Oh my god," I said, fumbling for a seat on the couch. "Oh my god."

My fears hadn't even gotten that far. I was so upset about losing Freddie and Ed that it never occurred to me that someone else would move in.

Or that a slumlord would buy Freddie's house and rent to college students who would throw parties on the deck three feet from my bedroom window every night.

Someone like my neighbor in Phoenix, who had fifty cats that all pooped in my yard and threw up worms on my front porch.

"I just hope they don't have chickens," my husband said as my head began to spin.

"Oh, shut up! If you say one more thing like that, I'm going to have to dose myself!" I said as my spine began to sweat and I tried to remember where I saw my bottle of Ativan last, which was prescribed for anxious and alarming situations exactly like this.

Exactly like chickens moving in next door to you.

Because this is what I think of having urban chickens in your backyard: YOU ARE AN ASSHOLE, AND YOUR FRIGGIN' CHICKENS ARE ASSHOLES. Yeah. That's what I said. I can see Safeway from my house. I can *see* it. And they have eggs at Safeway. Lots of eggs. White, brown, free-range, vegetarian-fed, organic, and plain-old-food-stamp eggs. Every kind of egg you might possibly want is already at Safeway. Already there, waiting for you to take them home. When you get your eggs from Safeway, you may not experience the joy of hunting them down in your backyard, but there's one thing you won't get: mice.

Mice that love the organic chicken feed you sprinkle around, mice that love the straw you put out for your fussy hens, mice that will then find their way into my house THAT IS THREE FEET FROM YOUR HOUSE and shit in my shoes. Because that's what mice do.

Eugene, Oregon, is a big DIY town. Everyone has a garden, most people are growing their own pot, and every other person on the street has made their own yogurt more than once. Some have died from it, but the herd is far from thinned. And see, the thing about making your own yogurt is that while it is also stupid, chances are that your neighbors don't know it because it does not necessarily require urban livestock unless you are a superasshole. When I lived in Phoenix, the only reason a goat was in someone's backyard was because there was going to be a barbecue later that night. In Eugene, urban farming is trendy, and these are the rules, according to Building Permit Services:

If the property is less than 20,000 square feet in area, any two of the following four categories of animals are allowed: 1. Chickens and Domestic Fowl (quails, pheasants, ducks, pigeons, and doves). Up to 6 over six months of age and 6 less than six months of age. No roosters, geese, peacocks, or turkeys allowed. 2. Rabbits. Up to 6 over six months of age and 6 less than six months of age. 3. Miniature Goats (pygmy, dwarf, and miniature goats). Up to 3 provided that males are neutered. 4. Miniature Pig. One up to 150 pounds. 5. Bees. Up to 3 hives as long as they are located at least 5 feet from all property lines. These standards are intended to improve the way animals are cared for, while increasing the likelihood that neighbors will accept your property uses and food choices.

Which means if you live anywhere, in any area, you can have a mini-farm. Like the lady down the street does, even though she doesn't have a backyard and her chickens roam freely, wandering in and out of traffic, wherever they please, pooping, peeing, and being dirty birds as far as they can waddle. Which begs the question: Why did the chicken cross the road? Because an asshole lady on Seventeenth and Willamette decided she needed a friggin' chicken friend. And not only can you raise farm animals; in your backyard, chickens, domestic fowl, and rabbits can be "harvested" right next to your swing set when I am on the chaise in my backyard, THREE FEET FROM YOU, reading a delightful book or throwing a nice little lunch party for my friends while the sounds of bunnies being slaughtered rises over and above the giggles we're having after a couple of mai tais.

And that's in addition to mice shitting in my shoes. If you know people who have raised chickens and they swear there's no mice around, it's because the shit balls roll right out of the holes in a Birkenstock, fall on the floor, and get combined with all of the other filth that's already there. I don't wear Birkenstocks. Some of my shoes are from Italy, shipped across an ocean *without being pirated,* deposited on a shelf for a year, and then placed on clearance at YOOX.com just to become a rodent toilet in my closet. If urban chicken farmers had shoes from Italy, they would know there is a problem. I have scientific proof, as documented below.

A CONVERSATION WITH MY FRIEND MARY

ME: How are you, Mary?
MARY: I found mice shit in my shoes.
ME: Do your neighbors have chickens?
MARY: Yes.

A CONVERSATION WITH MY FRIEND VALERIE

ME: How are you, Val?
VALERIE: My husband saw a rat in our kitchen.
ME: Do your neighbors have chickens?
VALERIE: Yes.

A CONVERSATION WITH MY FRIEND COLLEEN

ME: How are you, Colleen?
COLLEEN: I had chickens once. They were torn limb from wing by raccoons.

ME: You invited murder into your backyard. I'm
     sorry, that is not sad. But please remember to
     make sure to take whatever tortilla chip you
     touch. You have mouse shit hands. And most
     likely the hantavirus. Again, please stop touch-
     ing all the chips.

So yes, the thought of our new potential neighbors
was a bit of a worry spot for me, but I tried not to let it
show when I talked to Freddie. I wanted her to be excited for her new home and not dwell on the sadness that
would come with leaving the house she had raised her
children and grandchildren in. It was important to me
that she have a really good experience moving into her
new place.

"It's right around the corner from the good coffee shop
and the yarn store," she said happily. "Now I can walk
there!"

"That is awesome!" I said, nodding and smiling.
"Please don't sell the house to hippies. Patchouli makes
me nauseous. So does incense. And dream catchers."

Freddie laughed. "The backyard is so big," she added.
"We're going to build Ed an art studio back there."

"That is perfect!" I agreed. "And don't sell the house to
someone who might rent it to college kids."

"The house is such a manageable size, I can clean it in
about a half an hour!" she exclaimed.

"No way!" I chimed in. "Or to people with small children. Don't sell to people with small children. Older children or no children would be great."

"And did I tell you it's a stucco house?" she added. "That's not very common in Oregon."

"If you could find a nice, quiet retired couple, that would work out well," I suggested. "Without pets. Birds would be fine. As long as they don't put them out on the deck. Which is three feet from my bedroom window."

"I can't wait for you to come over and see it," she said with a wide, happy smile.

"A professor would be good," I suggested. "But not one from the folklore department. Everyone there is nuts."

Freddie kept on smiling.

I tried to, too.

"And try to get a good cook, if you can," I added. "Someone who brings vegan things or just carrots to the Fourth of July potluck won't go over well, I'm afraid. And not someone who thinks they make the best potato salad. We already have three of those, even though mine is clearly the winner. We could really use a skilled baker to round things out. A really good tiramisu would be excellent. Did I forget to mention no vegans?"

"No," Freddie answered. "You didn't."

A few weeks later the For Sale sign went up in Freddie's yard, the open houses began, and the prospective neighbors came.

"Ew," my husband said as we peered out from behind the curtains, watching them descend on the house. "God, I hope we don't get the one in the convertible Mercedes!"

"Oh my god," I agreed. "Meet me on the deck!"

We got out there in just enough time for the Mercedes people to step foot into Freddie's backyard.

"HONEY!" I yelled to my husband, who was ten inches from me. "That damn hobo pooped on our deck again!!"

"I bet he's still living in our next-door neighbors' bushes! The neighbors with the house for sale!" my husband yelled back.

"Perfect!" I whispered. "Wait! They're fleeing, but a van just pulled up with a rainbow painted on the side. Throw on that blue short-sleeved shirt I bought you and come back out here!"

"Why?" he asked.

"There is no time for questions when you have urban farmers entering the premises! Just do it!" I hissed.

Just as the van owners, both with waist-long stringy gray hair, passed an open window in Freddie's living room, I shouted, "Honey! How many people did you arrest on your shift today? I hope you got to shoot at a criminal! I love being married to a cop!"

Our next challenge was trying to anticipate scenarios and prepare for them before they actually occurred, like getting our telescope set up and clearly pointed toward Freddie's house should we see anyone undesirable, like people who looked like they might own a small yippy dog or raise their own lamb for Easter dinner. If I could have found a life-sized cutout of Gladys Kravitz, it would still be propped up in my window. But we barely had time to get the telescope up on three legs before Freddie came over with the news that she had sold the house.

"To a *family*?" I exclaimed, feeling for a soft place behind me to collapse. "I thought we covered that."

"They look very cute, and they sent me a picture of

themselves sitting on our front porch," she explained. "They look like the house was made for them. All of the children are adorable."

"All?" I said, putting my face in my hands. "How many?"

"I think three altogether," she replied. "I think you'll really like them!"

Four weeks later, Freddie and Ed had completely moved into their new stucco home with the huge backyard, and I had new neighbors. The three kids were running around the yard laughing when I walked up to their front door with a bunch of basil I had just pulled from my garden.

They were new to Oregon, just like we had been ten years before, and I could not have been more thankful that there wasn't a dream catcher or an item of tie-dye in sight. Mom drove a van, but it was a Toyota, not a Volkswagen, and as we made our introductions, the middle kid, a boy, ran over to the front porch where we were standing and tattled on his younger sister. "Mom! Lily is peeing on the side of the house!"

My new neighbor laughed exasperatedly, not the kind of laugh that said it was great that her kid was communing with nature or that it was adorable, but that her kid just peed on the side of the house and there wasn't much she could do about it now. I liked that.

"My house is a mess," she explained with a smile. "And I could say that it's just because we're moving in, but it's always going to look this way!"

"My house looks just like yours but I don't have kids," I said, and we both laughed. "And I'll tell you right now, although you are mainly going to see me in my bathrobe, I am not an alcoholic. Anymore."

"I wear mine when I take the kids to school," she divulged, and that's when I decided I liked our new family, a lot.

"Can we have Killer Burgers for dinner tonight?" Lily said as she ran around the corner from where she had just peed.

Then I decided that I loved them.

"I'm just so glad you didn't turn out to be the people with the rainbow-painted van," I said. "I was terrified they'd be our new neighbors. They looked like they were going to set up a chicken coop before they unpacked their dishes!"

My new neighbor laughed. "No, we didn't bring chickens with us all the way from Missouri," she said. "But I think we're going to get some."

"OH GOD PLEASE DON'T," I said before I even knew I was saying it. "They bring mice with them that poop in your shoes."

"Really?" my new neighbor said. "I never heard that."

"It's true," I said. "I swear it's true. I've done research. Everyone I know who has mice also has a neighbor with chickens."

She just nodded.

"Plus we have predators," I felt compelled to add, and pointed up toward a tree. "Raccoons."

"Freddie told us they were hit by a car," my neighbor replied.

"They got better," I said, nodding.

She nodded, too.

"And there are possums," I layered. "Possums have a hundred teeth. It will look like the Manson Family had a pillow fight back there."

Then it got quiet, despite the kids still laughing in the yard.

"How about if I buy you eggs every week?" I suggested. "I can even hide them in little spots all over your backyard like real chickens!"

My neighbor politely smiled and said nothing.

"Well, enjoy the basil," I said as I tried to smile again, and then walked back to my own house three feet away, wondering if people sold raccoons on Craigslist.

THE INCREDIBLE TRAVELS OF
SS LAURIE, THE DESTROYER

When I felt my big toe hit the cold water, I knew I had done something bad.

Really bad.

Awfully, truly, disastrously bad.

Why? I whined to myself. Why wasn't I paying attention? And why do I have to be naked?

Three days before, I had arrived in New York full of anticipation and excitement, eager to see what fun my trip with my friends Amy Si and Amy Se would bring. Since then, I had twirled a path of destruction and chaos that only a bad guest can.

I know I have the predilection to ruin things with a glance, obliterate an object with a step, and pulverize anything with a slight miscalculation. I try to restrain my Godzilla-like tendencies, but I'm fighting a losing battle, even without a swishing tail.

The more I try to be a good guest, the more I end up being not only a bad guest, but the reigning winner in the Bad Guest Hall of Fame. I bring my own booze so I don't drink yours. I bring my own food, too, especially salty snacks. I swear I will never go through your drawers. I will take you out to dinner. I will do your dishes. I will make my bed every day and try to control the encroaching spread of my possessions into your living area.

But I know myself better than that.

If I come to your house, I will spill a drink within the first ten minutes I am there. It doesn't matter if it's my drink or someone else's, my hands will find it and knock it over, especially if your table is set with heirloom linen from the old country or a brand-new, no-discounts-applied tablecloth from Gracious Home. If you have a pet, especially a small one or a kitten or puppy, I will terrify it by stepping on it before I see it and scar it forever. If I stay at your house for longer than twenty-four hours, I will clog your toilet just by peeing. And if I were dating you, the issue would be so bad that I would need to call you for help. Then you would break up with me.

And I totally get it.

My mother will be the first one to tell you what a horrible guest I am, even though I don't particularly consider myself a guest in my parents' house. Anywhere I may potentially live when I become broke enough doesn't meet the requirements, especially if at fifty, I still have a curfew of when I need to be "home."

Typically, every time I reenter the house after being away from it for an hour or two, I will open the front door and hear my mother say, "Laurie? Could you not leave your towel over the curtain rod? You're going to bring that whole goddamned thing down. It only stays up like that because of pressure and gravity."

"Laurie? Did you use the Keurig today? Because now it won't work."

"Laurie? Did you park on the wrong side of the street? Dad says you're going to get a ticket."

"Laurie? Could you please—" (gagging sounds) "There was a—" (more gagging sounds) "Oh my god. Oh my god—" (big gag) *"you left a hair on the sink!"*

"Laurie? There was a Hershey's chocolate Kiss right here on the counter. Did you see it?"

"Laurie? Did you leave a doody mark on the seat of the toilet?"

Yes. She actually asked me that. I'm not going to say who I suspected, but let me just mention that I had an eight-year-old nephew at the time who was recently learning to take care of things for himself.

The phone calls do not stop when I get home. I will inevitably open the front door after coming home from the airport to see that I have a message on my answering machine:

"Laurie? What is this? It's pink— *It's not pink? What the hell color is it then?* Dad says it's peach. *I don't think it's peach. You're crazy, this is peach? Go back upstairs. I'm leaving a message, Jimmy.* Anyway, your father found it in your room and we think it may be your underwear. It's long for underwear, though. It looks like it has legs. At first Dad thought it was a pile of skin. *Jimmy, I said go back upstairs.* Anyway, it's here. In case you are missing . . . skin. Yeah. I really don't like touching it. Don't ask me to mail it. I'm not sending underwear through the mail. That's illegal."

And after the following visit:

"Laurie? You left your girdle here again. At least this time Dad didn't try to kill it. It was behind the bed. Why are you throwing a girdle around in your bedroom? I don't understand what you were doing in there. I think that's very weird."

Now I hide a pair of Spanx somewhere in my parents' house every time I visit, and whoever finds it wins a prize.

But in New York, I swore I wouldn't leave anything behind, including hairs and broken shower curtain rods. I was not going to break, squash, or set anything on fire during my vacation, especially since Amy Si and I were staying at Amy Se's recently purchased apartment for a portion of the time.

Amy Si and Amy Se, by the way, have been best friends since first grade, as the teacher had them sit in alphabetical order, and both of their last names begin with *S*. To distinguish one from another, we add Si and Se, the next letter in both of their respective names, to avoid confusion and unnecessary blame.

Since Amy Si was a judge for a journalism award that takes place in a very swanky club in midtown, the foundation that hosts it provides complimentary quarters for three nights, which she shares with me because I tag along. It is the kind of place that makes me feel like a whore as soon as I walk into the lobby. I am not wearing pearls, I am not carrying Louis Vuitton luggage, and I am happy to pull my little suitcase behind me and not hand it over to the bellhop who desperately grabs for it, even though I just recently read in a vintage etiquette book that ladies should not carry their own luggage through hotel lobbies, lest they look like, well, a whore. I do not fit in here, and I never will.

One night, while staying at the club, I tried to hail a cab in the rain. I stepped off the curb where I didn't know there was a curb, fell right into the street, and when I got up, I had a big, round wet mark on my belly the size of a medium pizza.

"Oh! She's down!" the aging bellhop who watched the whole thing said to Amy Si, who was waiting inside. "One minute she was there, and the next it was like she was swallowed by a sinkhole."

But that was fine. I eventually gave him a dollar for hailing a cab while I wiped blood off of my knee.

I'm not exactly sure if it happened when I fell down, but the next day, I noticed a flopping noise coming from my foot that resulted in the discovery that the sole of my shoe had completely separated from the top. I found some Gorilla Glue at a nearby hardware store and tried to fix it, but unless I was going to stand on one foot for the next twenty minutes, the glue wasn't going to hold. I flopped around for the rest of the day, and that night I reapplied the glue and held it down with the leg of the nightstand on top of it. I am crafty that way. The next morning, Amy Si and I got up, had coffee and croissants, and mapped out all the places where we wanted to eat something that day. An hour later, we were showered and Amy Si was putting the finishing touches on her makeup in the bathroom, so I lifted the nightstand off my shoe and bent over to pick it up to see if the glue had held, but the shoe was ripped right out of my hand. I grabbed it again, and one more time, my hand came up empty.

Trying to figure out what was going on, I bent over to get a really good grip this time, and that's when I saw what looked like yellow goo bubbling out from my shoe and trailing all the way to the carpet.

Shit, I said to myself, then pulled as hard as I could on the shoe but it wasn't going anywhere. It was staying put, the sole of my shoe glued determinedly to the carpet. The Gorilla Glue had bubbled and expanded, growing to twice its size, and looking like honeycomb was bursting out of my shoe. I yanked again, no luck. I tried to shake it loose, but this was a fight I wasn't going to win without a knife.

Thank god for croissants, room service, and cutlery.

While Amy Si was still working on her eye shadow, I sawed away at that carpet like it was a leg that was trapped under a dislodged boulder and I was starting to get hungry.

Amy Si opened the door to find me sprawled out on the floor, working up a sweat.

"Are you doing yoga?" she asked incredulously.

"No," I huffed. "I glued my shoe to the carpet. Don't worry. I'll make sure that you can't tell so that you don't get charged for replacing the rug."

"Um," Amy Si said.

"I don't have a choice, Amy," I said as I stopped sawing

and looked up at her. "These are the only shoes I brought! I have to free them!"

She watched, not saying anything, as I chopped away at the carpet and freed the shoe, leaving a defiant bald spot where the attachment had been.

"Look," I said happily as I moved the leg of the nightstand over to cover the gaping patch of missing carpet. "You can't even tell!"

Amy opened her mouth and stayed like that for a long time until she said, "We might have to rearrange the room in order for no one to notice."

"I'm sure hundreds of Republicans have done very dirty things on this rug. It's time they replaced it anyway."

The next day, with the bed in our room moved over as far as it would go, we checked out of the club and brought all of our stuff over to Amy Se's.

"Please don't glue anything at Amy Se's," she said. "In fact, I'm going to need to hang on to that bottle until you leave for the airport."

Amy Se's new apartment was exquisite. Right off of Central Park West, it was in a gorgeous Art Deco building with beautiful windows, a gleaming wood floor, and a terrace that looked over her part of New York.

And I tried really, really hard to be good and watch myself and not break anything, down to the point that I covered my mouth when I brushed my teeth that night should any flecks of toothpaste try to fly out and land on the mirror.

That's how good I was being.

The next morning, I woke up feeling very victorious

that I had been in Amy Se's apartment for an entire twelve hours without backing up her plumbing or tearing a curtain rod out of the wall.

That is, until I turned over in bed and gasped at the pillowcase.

It looked like I'd had a tooth pulled overnight.

Sure, I had hand-guarded my mouth and watched where I stepped and used only the tiniest bits of toilet paper possible. But there was the evidence of Laurie, the Bad Houseguest, spread across the Frette linens in the form of bright red lipstick that my face had mushed all over it.

"Amy Se," I said as she headed out the door to work. "I ruined your very expensive pillowcase."

"Oh god," she laughed. "Don't worry about that. Bleach will take out everything."

"I will totally write you a check," I offered. "It will bounce the first time you put it through, but if you keep trying, the second or third time is usually the charm."

"You still write checks?" she asked.

"I'd go to the ATM but I can already tell you how that will turn out," I said. "At least with a check it looks like I'm making an effort."

"Really," she assured me. "Don't worry. It's only lipstick."

"I don't know what happened," I tried to explain. "I usually eat it all off by the end of the day."

"It's okay," she insisted as she walked out the door. "Have fun today!"

I tried to make up for my faux pas by doing all of her

dishes, but, to be honest, it was me who'd drunk out of all the glasses, as evidenced by the bright red lipstick on each rim.

Amy Si was still sleeping when I got into the shower, so I took my time, knowing there was no rush. Even Amy Se's bathroom was gorgeous, the original clawfoot bathtub surrounded by beautiful, original antique tiles.

When I finished my shower, I turned off the water and reached for a towel, and stepped onto the bathmat, which was strikingly cold as soon as my big toe hit it.

Squish.

Oh no.

Oh no, oh no, oh no, I cried to myself.

Oh, but yes.

An inch or more of water covered the entire floor of Amy Se's bathroom in enough of a flood that some biblical characters would start collecting animals. I had not made sure the shower curtain was all in the bathtub with me, and, as a result, my long, luxurious shower was now probably dripping onto the person in the shower below me.

I didn't know what to do. I was scared. I was horrified. I was naked.

I looked around and grabbed for a towel to throw on the floor like I would at my own house, but then I stopped. They were the most beautiful towels I had ever felt—soft, fluffy, absorbent, and utterly white. I got my towels at Restoration Hardware on clearance. I thought I had good towels. Amy Se's towels made my towels feel like dried-up leaves. There was no way I was going to ruin any more of her white things, so instead I wrapped one around me and did what I know only bad guests do: started pokin' around.

I opened doors, closets, drawers—anything that had a handle on it, I opened it. I found her mop in the hallway closet, and quickly tiptoed back to the bathroom, leaving a trail of water behind me. Then I mopped and I squeezed, and I mopped and I squeezed, and I mopped and I squeezed, and twenty minutes later, when I had mopped up what had to be gallons and gallons of water, I got dressed and opened the bathroom door to find Amy Si awake and walking toward me.

She stopped in her tracks.

"What did you do?" she asked me point-blank when she saw the mop in my hand. "How much of the floor is missing in there?"

"None," I said quickly. "Not a bit. Not a bit. I just spilled some water, so while I had the mop I figured I'd just wash the floor."

"Really?" she asked me. "Is that all?"

"Yep," I answered honestly. "It was only water. I promise."

"Okay," she said, then smiled. "I did some cleaning, too, last night. Someone left chocolate on the toilet seat!"

I WILL SURVIVE. HEY HEY.

When I came down the stairs one morning not very long ago, I was met with an angry-faced husband who waited until I had fully entered the kitchen before exclaiming, "Do you know when that peanut butter expired?" pointing to the jar of Skippy on the counter.

I had no idea. "I need to have coffee and get some pants on before I fully commit to acting as a peanut butter psychic," I said. "Or you could save me the trouble of trying to shove these slippers through pajama bottoms, getting them stuck, then spending the next ten minutes kicking my way through the foot hole, and just tell me."

"*Nine years,*" he proclaimed, as if those words could part a violent sea. "That is older than our car!"

"Please don't eat the car," I responded with a smile, but to no avail.

"Do you know what nine-year-old peanut butter tastes like?" my husband questioned again.

Personally, I guessed it was not very good after I grabbed the jar out of the cupboard last night and tried to give some to the dog, who was being extra picky, though it was now apparent she used her senses for carbon dating.

"No, but I do know what Purina Puppy Chow in the can tastes like," I offered as a consolation.

"That's because you eat everything brown you see that's lying around, thinking that it's chocolate!" he replied.

"Yes, I told you, I thought it was double-chocolate cookie dough with coconut in it on the kitchen counter," I tried to explain.

"Had you made cookie dough in the recent past, or know why a lump of cookie dough would be on the kitchen counter? By itself? With no other cookie dough around it?" he questioned.

"No, but as I've told you before, sometimes you have to take that risk, because it could have turned out to be chocolate instead of dog food. You never know. It would have haunted me forever," I concluded. "Sometimes, you win."

"But most times in this house, you don't," my husband interjected. "Most times you put a spoonful of honey and peanut butter mixed together into your mouth expecting a win with a wonderful salty sweet treat, but you lose with a wave of sticky, unspit-outable, rancid peanut flavor accompanied by the burn of gasoline."

"You know," I started, pretty boldly for a fat girl who hadn't shaved her legs since summer, "I buy a lot of peanut butter. You *eat* a lot of peanut butter. There is no alarm that goes off on peanut butter when it expires. It is not my fault that Skippy has not changed its label since

2007. And believe me, you may turn your nose up at almost adolescent-aged peanut butter now, but after the apocalypse, you will scoop that shit out and eat it with your fingers. It's staying in the cabinet."

Then I got my coffee and went upstairs to get my pants on before he started checking expiration dates on other things in the pantry.

I remember the glory days of my Y2K prep like it was yesterday. I was there for every sale of canned creamed corn, three for a dollar. I had enough beef jerky to keep the Donner Party from eating their neighbor's rump roast. I had cases of Hormel chili and beef stew hidden in closets for when the starving mobs came to raid us. I had twenty jars of peanut butter, one of which my husband might have just eaten. I did it for that man. The man who was laughing at me now and who laughed at me then for keeping cans of tuna fish in my shoes. But then, as I would still say now, when disaster strikes and your tum-tum has been empty for several days, *mi esposo,* you'll chow down on rancid peanut butter like it was a Milky Way bar, and then after you get violently ill from it, you'll do it all over again when the next hunger pang hits.

Preparing for an emergency doesn't take much; all you really need is just a little foresight and the will to live. That's about it. I've tried to consider everything.

The first thing to do is determine what type of emergency you might face, because the details of preparedness may vary. In epidemic/plague conditions, yeah, you're probably going to die no matter how many cans of creamed corn you have hidden behind the water heater.

Somewhere along the line, you're going to touch a contaminated poop hand and die the same grueling death as the rest of the population. If you don't, well then, you can thank the likes of people like me who can smell a disaster like the brilliant scientists in movies that no one ever listens to. The plus side is that half of the IRS will be dead, getting a cab will be easier, and maybe people will start washing their hands for a goddamned change.

In the event of acts of God, I like to think I've gotten my training from owning the DVD of *2012*, which depicts in startling accuracy this very scenario, and although I do believe I could probably drive a limousine through a highrise glass building, I'm not so sure about the skills necessary to fly a plane during the creation of thousands of volcanoes and meteor showers while the Earth's crust collapses below me. That's a rather large scope. However, if I can make it through that, this is the day of reckoning for all of the chubby people who have wisely stored their reserves for precisely this purpose. The chubs have come home to roost. All of the girls with polycystic ovarian syndrome (of which I am one) will emerge the victors in the race for survival. For all of us who couldn't lose weight if we were in a North Korean prison camp, this is our moment. This is what we were made for. Most of us are barren and will resume our marsupial-like coating once electrolysis is inaccessible, but the human race doesn't need to live on. *We* do.

Now although I don't necessarily believe in monsters, and the chances are relatively slim for a dormant creature to suddenly waken and start smashing the landscape, the fact of the matter is that it's not a hundred percent that it can't happen. Should we experience a contagion of devils, an army of alien beings, or a sudden barrage of anything we don't understand but have read about in a Stephen King book, I plan on clambering to the highest point I can find and simply jumping off, or eating everything I have in dented cans. Personally, I don't want to wait to discover firsthand if the enemy eats people and then suddenly find there's a fang in my intestines. I don't think I want to live until the end of this movie. Likewise, it's unfair to dangle the thin string of hope here, but if there is one bright spot, it's that everyone who ever wronged you, told the entire girls' PE class that you had a camel toe, or spread the rumor that you were not psychic as you claimed to be at the slumber party, is dead. And that probably means Matthew McConaughey, too.

Now, the apocalypse I'm most prepared for is nuclear holocaust since I watched *The Day After,* a made-for-TV movie that everyone in this country watched one night in 1983 and that turned me into a spooker forever. I blame that movie, hands down, for my Y2K mania, and after waiting seventeen years for a reason to stockpile anything, I was eager to put into place the lessons I had learned from JoBeth Williams and Jason Robards as they faced eternity in a basement. Nuclear holocaust, the shadow that hung over the childhoods of the eighties—even more so than the horrific "We Built This City" by Starship—is always a threat, always a possibility. It only takes one despot who's stepped off his meds to cause nuclear annihilation. Frankly, I don't want to be incinerated by a lunatic who shoots at whales with a crossbow (yes, Vladimir, I'm talking to YOU).

I already have a basement, so I am one shelter ahead of the game. Chances are I'll have been vaporized, although I really don't know why any insane despot would target Eugene, Oregon, unless they hated hippies, which on second thought is an excellent reason to target Eugene, Oregon. I once knew a girl who was determined to save all trees by eliminating toilet paper from use, and if you had to tinkle when in her hovel of a home, then that applied to you, too. After you were done answering nature's call, there were pee rags—old washcloths, dishcloths, and assorted pieces of former clothing—in a dirty basket that your hostess, who once woke up with rats GNAWING ON HER HAIR, had provided for your "needs." Simply wipe yourself with one and deposit it in the basket on the other side of the toilet. I don't think I need to say it, but anyone who wakes up with a rat eating part of them is probably not too concerned about washing pee rags in a sanitary manner. I'm sure that basket was a grab bag of chlamydia, gonorrhea, and all 114 varieties of HPV. I also knew someone with herpes who left their sex toys—which I don't think were being run through the sterilization cycle, either—out in the open and within reach of children. So by all means, someone put Eugene, Oregon, on the nuke map. Even before Los Alamos. Put a red circle here, Vlad.

I'm finding it essential to move on here. I have assembled a short-but-pointed list of things I will need in The Hole (which is what I will begin calling my basement when the End Days come), and although these items fit my personal needs, I believe them to be universal as well:

- A pillow: Ever try to sleep on a plane without a pillow? Now try sleeping in a shelter without one. It will also be a good therapeutic tool when the need to scream becomes uncontrollable.
- Matches in a waterproof container: Essential when your potty is about a foot away from your bed.
- Pictures of food you will never eat again: Bringing back good memories of your previous life can be cheery and morale boosting. What makes a smile appear like a plate of chicken Parmesan?
- Hair of loved ones who have passed before you, most likely before your very eyes: Collect the hair and fashion it until you have something resembling a Grief Doll.

No one really survives an apocalypse alone, so I believe it is essential to fashion a sort of survival team, but this is something that must be curated with careful thought and insight. Sure, my father-in-law is funny, but when it comes to providing a useful skill in the effort of your survival, chuckles are worthless. You have to earn your place in my Hole. It is important when choosing your Survival Team to assemble people of good cheer, fast runners, and those without gastrointestinal problems or food allergies. Even though the apocalypse diet rarely contains meat, do not allow vegans onto your Survival Team unless it is for the specific purpose of possibly consuming them later on if things turn super shitty. This way there's no guilt, and other members of the Survival Team will be clamoring to tap them on the head with a sizeable rock.

After careful consideration, I believe these are the spots I need to fill:

- DOCTOR: Most essential of all spots. You'll need a touch of help should things turn a bit for the worse, such as should your intestines start dragging on the ground behind you or your skin begin falling off in large sheets. (Note: A midwife is NOT a doctor. A doula is NOT a doctor. A person who has given birth at home in a baby pool is NOT a doctor. A physician's assistant is NOT a doctor, but will suffice if you only know people who have graduated from community college.)
- BACKUP DOCTOR: In case something should befall the first doctor. Like death. Or if they are revealed as a vegan.
- THE MUSHROOM GUY: Mushrooms will probably become very large and bountiful after a nuclear holocaust, but every mushroom has an evil twin. You may be chowing down on a luscious portobello only to discover six hours later that your kidneys said "No way!" and you're being tossed into a shallow grave by morning. You can typically recruit Mushroom Guys at farmer's markets, brew festivals, and acoustic nights. Look for a fellow who is rather unkempt, bears an earthy essence, or drives

a VW van that uses biofuel. And has a sticker on the back window that says so.

- AN OUTDOORSMAN: Ideally, this should be someone who has experience in the wilderness, but in places where people only wear the accoutrements of such a person, like in Brooklyn, a person who has been camping will suffice, preferably in a tent and not in an RV. This person will hopefully know north from south, but if you're really in a bind to find one, a homeless person will pretty much do.
- THE PROFESSOR: Someone who can produce a bike that makes electricity and a radio out of coconuts.
- A VINTNER: The only hope you will have in the foreseeable future.
- SCAPEGOAT: An IT person would be spectacular for this role, or a gamer. Someone bearing nominal interpersonal skills, who will mainly keep to themselves but will provide an immeasurably valid role when the hunt is fruitless and the waste bucket needs emptying while fallout is still drifting like snow. Usually, this role is the first to be vacated.

Those who will not be making my Survival Team include: lawyers, accountants, actors, poets, salespeople, baristas, city council members, magicians, or those with guitars. Simply put, none of these folks have anything to offer in survival experience. Most of these types are needy, do not require a lot of quiet time, and might even jeopardize your very existence by humming a jaunty tune, nervously jiggling their foot, or unconsciously shouting out orders when a troop of alien scouts, a hive of radiated super bees, or a white supremacist, who has survived everything while wearing merely a tank top, is hovering nearby.

If I do, indeed, survive the nuclear holocaust, I realize I might notice several aftereffects of being cooked like a hot dog. These may include a slight headache, a little wooziness, some extra pooping, and regular ol' hair loss. I'll see it in just about everybody. A little on the sides, a little off the top, a clump here or there. I'll try to think of it as a bonus; I will now have the supplies I'll need to add to my family of Grief Dolls.

If I make it that far, the day will come that I notice I'm bleeding from places that don't normally bleed, or that my intestines are hanging a little lower outside of my body than typical. I'm planning on taking this opportunity to start making a bucket list of the enjoyable activities I'd like to accomplish within, say, the next fifteen minutes. I might try gazing at a nuclear sunset, or leaving my extra skin on the pillow of the person I loathe the most on the Survival Team. But there's good news, too. I can leave The Hole now, with my fingers scooping from a jar of rancid peanut butter.

THE HAM-OFF

I looked her straight in the eye. She looked straight back.

There was going to be a battle.

Because I'm serious about my ham.

I had three kids to feed, plus my husband, myself, and our rafting guide, so I knew precisely what I needed and how much. Besides, it had been an exhausting twenty minutes just trying to navigate my way through the store over to the deli section. And this was at the fancy grocery store, where things like this weren't supposed to happen.

I don't know how to better demonstrate the devolution of the human species than by tracking grocery store etiquette.

There's always been a problem at Costco. It was our first indication that our thumbs were de-opposing back into the forms of monkey hands. Costco, however, creates most of its own problems; when you hand out, for free, teaspoons of Campbell's cream of mushroom soup and quarters of a chicken nugget, you have to expect mayhem.

People will do anything for free food, no matter how minuscule.

I've done it myself. I will wholly admit that I have stood in line there waiting for a piece of pizza half the size of a business card, and when an eight-year-old cut in front of me and grabbed two slices, saying, "One is for my dad," I mumbled, "I bet you don't even *have* a dad."

I thought shopping in the fancy grocery store would be safer; I was recently run out of our closest Safeway when the nearby university enrolled ten thousand more students than the previous year. I should have seen it coming. Countless baby birds, their mouths agape and on their own for the first time in their lives, wandered up and down the aisles with a grown-up cart (no Playskool car attached) like zombies, unsure what to say, do, or reach for. It was as if they had been transferred here from another planet in which the dirty secrets of domestic requirements to ensure the duration of one's life were carefully hidden from them by well-meaning but utterly failing parents.

Mothers and fathers: If you want to do one thing that will prepare your child for his first time away from home at college, don't buy him matching sheet sets, and don't supply him with sweatshirts with his college logo; take him to the goddamned grocery store. I know your child thinks that food just appears, comes through the mail, or is delivered by a grocery Santa, but take a moment to show him the basics. This way I won't have to nearly gore your kid with my cart and a strategically placed baguette when he's blocking the part of the freezer section I need to get my Tater Tots from because he's on the phone with you, asking how to make Eggo waffles.

I couldn't take Safeway anymore. Between navigating the jammed aisles of feckless teenaged shufflers and waiting in the pharmacy line to get my Ativan Rx behind seventeen college students trying to get meningitis shots, I had had it. The parking lot had been reduced to a game of duck-duck-goose, and I'm simply too old to stand behind a frat guy in the express lane who is buying enough frozen pizza and cheap beer to bring at least three pledges relatively close to death. I can't wait for him to learn how to count beyond nine when I need to tear open the package of Poise Roll-On Cooling Gel that is in my hands and apply it NOW.

I thought things would be better at the fancy grocery store a mile up the road. But do you know who shops there? The parents who have sent their kids away to colleges in other states to infiltrate and destroy the neighborhood grocery stores there. There are times when I have had to talk myself down in that store, aloud. I know that sounds crazy, but I want to spend as little time in that madness as possible. I don't want to compare yogurts. I don't need to hover over the cheese section like a UFO. I would actually pay a premium to shop there at an allocated time reserved for people who can pass a certain level of efficiency. You'd have to take a test. I would pass it. Questions would include: "Draw the shortest path between eggs, milk, and bread"; "What is the difference between fat-free, one percent, two percent, and whole milk without looking at the label?"; "Which of these tomatoes is a Roma?"; and "The Doritos are on the right side of the snack aisle. Do you leave your cart a) on the left side, b) at the end of the aisle, c) on the right side, hugging as close to that side as possible without knocking things off the shelf, or d) Why is there a wrong side?"

It never fails. Every time I go to the grocery store, even the fancy one, I see adults wandering about in a cloud of stupor, not sure where they are going, confused as to where they've been, abandoning their carts and leaping in front of mine to get a half-inch free sample of domestic Swiss cheese.

It makes me think, Who feeds you? Who dresses you in the morning? Because those are surely more complex activities than picking up a dozen eggs without difficulty, yet you don't seem to be able to conquer *that* feat. Do you know who the kid who called his mom about Eggo waffles grows up to be? The dad with two unruly children who, again, stands in front of the freezer section I need, reading the ingredients on every box of meatless burger on the shelves. Want to know what's in a Gardenburger? Google it. They have a website, I promise. Try to do your legwork at home, and fill up on tiny squares of shitty cheese before you get to the store. Make a ninety-nine-cent crappy pizza, cut it into fifty pieces, and have a friggin' sample fest yourself.

I had dealt with all of this inertia for twenty minutes already at the fancy grocery store, buying chips, soda, and snacks for our river-rafting trip the next day. My nieces and nephew were visiting from Arizona, I knew exactly what I needed, and I didn't want to take an ounce or slice less than what was required for everyone to get the sandwich they desired.

I finally got to the deli counter, and ordered a quarter pound of ham sliced thin from the girl working there. And this is what I want to say to her:

Dear little teenager working in the deli at Market of Choice who just cut my ham: When I ask you for a quarter pound, and I can see from the scale that you only gave me twenty-two percent and now are attempting to wrap it up, I am going to mention this. The right answer is not to tell me that twenty-two percent is a quarter pound, because it's not. Your next move should not be insisting that twenty-two percent IS a quarter pound, because although I went to college a long time ago and was drunk for most of it, I remember that a quarter pound is twenty-five percent because my boyfriend used to sell drugs. And I know that if you sell someone a quarter pound of pot and only give them twenty-two percent, the biker who just gave you cash is going to come back and set your house on fire. And I feel the same way about ham.

"It's not a quarter pound," I said, staring her right in the eye.

"So you want more than a quarter?" she asked.

"I do not," I replied. "I want what I asked for. A quarter pound."

"Fine," she snapped, grabbed the ham off the scale, and returned to the slicer.

Then she came back with three quarters of a pound, ham sliced so thick I could have laid it as tile.

"How is that?" she asked with a smirk.

"That is perfect," I smirked back, and she wrapped it up, then took off her little chef's hat, slapped it down on the back table, and walked out of view.

Her co-worker stepped up and asked if I needed anything else.

"Actually, I do," I informed her. "I need you to tell me that you know that twenty-five percent is a quarter pound, right? You know that, I know you do. You look like you do. So please, please tell me that you know that a quarter pound is not twenty-two percent."

"If you will permit me to speak," she said with an attitude I did not particularly care for, "it's within our Market of Choice guidelines that twenty-two percent is a quarter pound."

"Twenty-two percent of a pound is *not* a quarter," I repeated. "Just like if I asked you for change for a twenty-dollar bill and a five, you couldn't give me two tens and two ones. Even I know that, and the left side of my brain is basically an empty walnut shell."

She pinched her furry little mouth together in a twisted knot and was barely able to get out "Is there anything else I can do for you?"

And I stood there, and stood there, and stood there, and instead of retracting my opposable thumb and going apeshit on her, I reached into my cart and slapped the ham tiles back onto her counter and said, "Yeah. You can have your twenty-two percent back."

Then, because I was tired, because I was angry, and because I know what twenty-five percent is, I found the manager and informed him that poor math skills were poisoning his deli.

"And here's a hint," I said before I left. "If your employees are so bad at math that they are goading your customers into a ham-off, the least you could do is put some free cheese cubes up there."

THE DAY I GREW
A SECOND HEAD

With a gasp, I realized that I was never going to be able to wear a tube top again.

The birth of my second head was slow; it never announced itself with a pinch of pain, an ache, or the pull of a contraction. Instead, it slowly began to appear, unnoticeable at first, building itself in secrecy until it produced a slight, extra curve that I proudly identified as muscle.

Lookit that, I thought. The image in the mirror didn't lie—my trapezius muscle (while I had failed biology in both high school and college, I never failed Google) was blooming; it had a nice delicate arc to it, representative of domestic weight training, or what I call lifting grocery bags and putting dishes back on the shelf. It made complete sense to me that it was limited to my right side; Twizzlers may not weigh much individually, but when you're lifting them up in tiny increments to your mouth in a repeated motion for most of the afternoon, that's basically equivalent to lying in a smelly basement, curling a five-pounder a couple of times.

It *is*.

Plus, I stir coffee with that hand, put on makeup with that hand, and butter bread with that hand. It all adds up, I thought logically; I'll butter anything. What did I expect? I asked myself. I'm an active person. Of course I'm going to see results from that!

I was contemplating using my left hand for chips and dip to even out my muscular progression when I put my purse strap over my right shoulder, where it had always gone, and I felt something odd. It felt weird. Un-right.

It felt like something in my neck had moved. Alarmed, I reached back to investigate and, to my horror, realized it was true, as I pressed my neck with my fingers and felt them slip an inch downward.

Which was not good. I already have too many parts of my body that barely fit together. When you're trying on boots in a snotty department store, in front of a salesman who already doubts your shoe size just by your gait, it does not help if your kneecap switches sides like it's a red square on a Rubik's Cube. When you've dodged out of a crowded performance of *A Midsummer Night's Dream* to use the potty, and snuck back in past the sentries who stop you and insist you wait until halftime, it's preferable that your right hip doesn't click noticeably with every step like the snapping fingers of the Jets getting ready to rumble with the Sharks as you try to steal back to your seat.

I prefer my body parts to remain in the area to which

they have been assigned. I understand it must be boring to repeat the same function over and over again, but I have no idea where my trapezius muscle thought it was going to escape to when it started sliding down my back. The last thing I needed was for it to cross the border into Assland, where it was already overcrowded. Assland is accepting no more transfers, I decided. We have reached our quota in those hills. So I brought it up on my next appointment with my knee doctor after I cried pain tears in Nordstrom's shoe department when my kneecap revolved like the moon around the Earth.

"I think one of my muscles got dislocated," I mentioned as he was about to wrap up my exam. "It's kind of sliding off the bone. Like meat in a slow cooker."

He looked at me as if I had just thrown a handful of glitter into the air and exclaimed that I could grow beans in my nose.

"I think you need a different kind of doctor," he said before he left.

I translated that professional medical opinion into meaning that I was perfectly fine and need not worry about sections of my body succumbing to gravity, even if that gravity was acting more like a black hole. But despite the fact that the muscle in my neck was headed for a free fall, it kept getting bigger and more pronounced. I decided to bring it up to the physical therapist who was treating my knee.

"It's probably because you carry such a heavy purse," she said after squeezing the crook between my neck and my shoulder. "You have a lot of snacks in there. You're just super strong on that side. Nothing to worry about. Probably."

"But don't you feel how it's kind of moving?" I asked. "It's a little like a water weenie."

As if she had psychic abilities and could tell where I had been, she immediately shot away from me like I was a power outlet and she was a butter knife.

"It is a little like a jelly doughnut. I would try carrying your purse on the other side," she said quietly. "Or take out one of those Pepsi bottles."

I winced and slightly shook my head. "You never know when you're going to get lost on a logging road and have to lick the condensation off your windshield five days in," I replied. "Birds shit on that thing. I'll just put my purse on the other side."

So I did, but three weeks later, my other side hadn't gotten any bigger. It was still just flat, and I mentioned that to my friend Mary when I was at her house for a barbecue.

"What do you mean by 'water weenie'?" she asked.

"Some people prefer 'jelly doughnut,'" I tried to explain.

Before I knew it, Mary's hand was on my shoulder, pushing down.

"That's a lipoma," she said as she went back to opening the pack of hot dogs. "So now you can stop saying 'like meat in a slow cooker.'"

I just looked at her, not really understanding. Mary is a doctor, and not of poetry. She was the valedictorian of her graduating class and accidentally tripped and knocked down an elderly Francis Crick, the co-discoverer of the structure of the DNA molecule and the keynote speaker at the ceremony, in the process. I just forget Mary is smart and a medical professional. She wears Converse a lot.

"It's a tumor," she explained. "I doubt it's cancer, though."

"Lipoma means 'second head' in Latin, doesn't it?" I said, suddenly feeling not so strong. "I always had a feeling I ate my twin. Another stomach would explain everything."

"If you ate your twin, it's probably because it was an asshole," Mary said. "It's just a fatty tumor, people get them in middle age. Nothing to be worried about. Unless it gets bigger."

I know that I'm middle-aged; I know that. I was not shocked to hear it. I am pleased that I defied nature this long to grow old enough to have a middle-age-appropriate tumor. When I was twenty-seven and woke up one morning after hitting my head on the railroad tracks but was more upset about spilling my Jack and Coke, no one would have predicted that I would outlive Amy Winehouse. But I did outlive her. I'm old enough for gray hair, arthritis, and, apparently, second heads that I was sure had a genome comprised of Twinkie fluff and whatever toxic waste makes Funyuns so alluringly crunchy.

It was the "unless it gets bigger" amendment that shocked me. I was too busy concentrating on conjuring up another matching tumor for my left side to contemplate that the one I already had would get even bigger.

How much bigger would it get? I wondered. So big it

would act like a built-in neck pillow for airplanes? What exactly were the parameters on this? Was I going to have to start wearing a scarf? Did I need to start introducing it? Should I name it?

Oh god. I didn't want to be that person. The goiter lady. I am already too frighteningly close to any character Pixar has put into cat-eye glasses. I've called a truce with my rapidly rippling skin and the white goat hairs on my chin. But a hump? I can be eccentric. Eccentric is fine because eventually, people just expect you to eat all the cheese at parties and then fall asleep in an armchair with your legs open. But there was no way I was going to star in my own sideshow. Yes, I need a Plan B to see me through until retirement age, but riding that wave on a mountain range rumbling out of my neck was not what I had envisioned. Now my choices had bubbled down to the circus or working in an elementary school as a lunch lady.

It might not be so bad, I tried to tell myself. Everything has its bright side, right? After all, I could live in a Gypsy wagon and start telling fortunes to stupid people, or I could move into a gingerbread house and be legitimately expected to steal candy from children. I might enjoy life as a forest witch. You never know. The hump would make me terrifying, especially if I put a hat on it and gave it some lipstick. Those kids would drop those Milky Way bars before I even had to shriek or put them in an oven.

Or I could hit the stand-up circuit, invite Louis C.K. and Ira Glass, and open my act with "My name is *Laurie* Notaro. I don't have cancer. But I do have this tumor! Sorry to have gotten your hopes up."

"Don't worry," Mary said when she noticed I didn't ask for seconds of dessert. "I know a good surgeon."

Dr. Henderson was a nice lady, mainly because she didn't recoil in horror when I revealed the second head.

"No problem," she said, as if she touched disgusting things on people all day. "It's about five centimeters big."

"I'm an American," I reminded her.

"As big as an apricot," she clarified.

I shuddered, but then became instantly hopeful.

"How much do you think it weighs?" I said excitedly, thinking that the tumor might have the density and weight of plutonium or a particle from a neutron star. "That could answer a lot of questions for me."

"Weighs as much as an apricot," she said without looking up. "Let's get you in next week!"

Hoping it was in the ninety-ninth percentile for apricots and I might effortlessly lose a pound, I agreed.

"If this second head starts talking when I'm on the table," I said earnestly to my doctor, "just pull the plug. Do the merciful thing. That's not the kind of life I want to live. And if it calls you an asshole for sticking a knife in it, it's not my responsibility. It didn't come from my mouth."

The day before my surgery, I realized I had broken Notaro family law by not milking every second of attention possible out of my tumor. I hadn't told anybody. What was I thinking? I laughed as I got out my phone and texted my sisters and my mom. Maybe someone might send me a gift card! I upgraded the fruit of my tumor just in case.

"I'm having surgery tomorrow," I tapped away. "It's no big deal. I have a tumor (size of a large plum!!!) growing out of my neck like an unborn twin. They are almost 100 percent sure it's not malignant. So it's nothing to worry about. Day surgery, in and out. I am terrified each morning when I get up that it's sprouted an eye or, worse, a mouth. But if I die, my husband gets the life insurance policy, but if for some reason he dies at the same time tomorrow, split it between the kids. Don't get any ideas. Talk soon."

Ready to answer a barrage of panicked texts, I stretched and warmed up my fingers and got ready for the long haul.

And then, an hour later, my sister replied with a single word.

"Shit," she said.

"No, it's fine," I pecked hungrily, eager to quell her unignorable thoughts of tragedy and her angry threats to God to make this right. "I promise. It's not cancer. I am pretty sure that I got it from carrying that heavy purse."

Send.

I sat for fifteen minutes before I realized her answer had another meaning.

"Or is it 'Shit, I thought I was getting the money'?" I wrote.

Send.

When she apparently got back from lunch, she took a moment out of her obviously packed schedule to text back to her sister, who very well may have had cancer, to say, "Shit, you have an evil twin growing on your neck."

This time, I waited for a while before I answered.

"What did you expect?" I furiously jabbed precisely forty-five seconds later. "Mom smoked and ate a lot of Chinese food. We all have an Emily somewhere."

Send.

"Damnit. Evil twin, not Emily. Evil twin! HATE autocorrect."

Send.

My mother and my other sister, I was sure, were someplace together, eating Chinese food and laughing about Emily as their phones emitted "Wind Beneath My Wings" and the sounds of crashing waves in tandem.

"Like she didn't smoke herself!" I could hear my mother say as she slurped from her wonton soup. "Sure, blame it all on me. Maybe it's all the LSD pills she took. See? *I was right*. I knew she wasn't just drunk all those times!"

"I put this curse on her in 1978 when she ate the last brownie you made for her birthday," my sister Linda added as she bit into an egg roll, a drip of sweet-and-sour sauce hitting her plate with a splash. "I even wrote my initials on it. She ate it anyway. Been waiting for this day for a long time."

The next day, I checked in for surgery, and I had to answer some questions from the nurse beforehand.

"Have you ever had surgery before?" she asked, her pen and notepad poised.

"Yes," I answered.

"How many times and for what?" she asked.

"Wisdom teeth, gallbladder removed, and another time," I said quickly.

"What was the last one for?" she queried.

"Well, I'm, well—it was something to do with my, um, my . . ." I trailed off, hoping the nurse would give up.

She just looked at me.

"My lady parts," I said, looking away.

"Hysterectomy?" she asked.

"No, no, just a cervical thing," I replied.

"What kind of thing?" she continued.

"I'm not sure, I wasn't awake, but it involved irregular cells," I offered.

"HPV?" she asked.

I drew a breath and then stopped.

"I came 'of age' in the nineties," I explained. "I'm not sure."

"HPV." She nodded and scribbled something down on the pad.

Great. Now it's down on paper somewhere. Laurie N. possibly had a dirty disease. I finally and truly understood the meaning of the word "apeshit." As my stomach suddenly curled, cramped, and threatened, I wanted nothing more than to start knocking things over with frantic arms and scream while I swung the pants that I had just crapped in over my head like a monkey helicopter.

"Are you Laurie Notaro, the writer?" she asked.

I just went numb. Had I known, I thought to myself, had I known this moment would arrive, I would have named the hump Emily and lived happily ever after in a hut in the forest with my oven always on broil.

"You know," I said as calmly as possible, "maybe you

should have switched the order of those last two questions."

In an hour I was unconscious and in a vulnerable position not wearing underwear in front of people I didn't know who were told not to let their hands dip below my navel on one side or my crack on the other.

"She was a nineties girl," I'm sure they snickered. "Even alcohol won't kill that. Only fire is sufficient."

When I slogged to the surface hours later, the first thing I saw was my husband standing next to the bed.

". . . were two sets of hands in your body," I thought I heard him say, to which I thought, I hope they wore gloves. I hope they wore gloves. No one wore gloves in the nineties but Michael Jackson.

As it turned out, they did, but the location of the invasion was slightly different than I had envisioned. Apparently, my second head was sneaky, and like the Loch Ness monster, had carefully hidden the bulk of its size beneath the darkness. Emily, it turned out, was not an apricot; she was not a plum, she was not an orange, she was a grapefruit.

A grapefruit that was beginning to wrap herself around my lung.

"I got in there with both hands," Dr. Henderson recounted excitedly for me during my follow-up visit, my neck purple and stapled. "And I pulled and I pulled, but it was enormous! I had to call another doctor in, and we both had our hands in there, pulling as hard as we could!"

"That is so gross" was all I could say.

"But I got it!" she said with the smile of victory. "And when I got it all out, I couldn't believe the size. I had never seen one that big before."

"I thought I had been getting pretty strong," I tried to explain.

"I took a picture of it!" she said, beaming. "And I put it in the book!"

"What book?" I asked. Please, I thought to myself. Don't say it. Don't say it.

"The book I show my students of medical oddities," she exclaimed.

She had said it.

I had made the circus after all.

"The scar will be longer than I told you," she added. "We had to make it bigger."

"For both sets of hands," I finished.

"For both sets of hands," she agreed. "That's never happened before! Four hands! I thought the incision would be six inches, but it's about nine. I'm sorry."

No more tube tops for this girl.

"It's all right," I said as I felt the row of staples with my fingers like they were piano keys. "When people see it and ask me what happened, I'm going to tell them I got it when I got caught in a civil war in Africa."

She looked at me curiously.

"Think of the children I can scare," I added, and already felt my stomach growling.

SCATTERED, COVERED, AND SMOTHERED: THE INFINITE WISDOM OF WAFFLE HOUSE

I was setting the table for dinner at Nana's house when I heard a small voice call out from deep in the hallway.

"Aunt Laurie?" eight-year-old Nicholas called out. "Would you help me?"

"Sure, Bub," I replied, and headed down the hall to the bathroom, where he sat on the potty, swinging his legs.

"I need help," he said matter-of-factly.

"What's the matter?" I asked, seeing nothing amiss. "Are you out of toilet paper?"

He looked at me and seemed puzzled. "No," he said, shaking his head.

"Then what's wrong?" I asked.

He looked at me like I was stupid. His expression contained a hint of disgust, but was comprised mainly of confusion and wonder that I had grown to be this tall and was so oblivious to the issue.

"Wipe me," he said starkly, scrunching his eyebrows with annoyance that he actually had to provide me with the answer.

Now, I had a choice here. Either I could express my utter revulsion and shock at his request, or I could act my height and do the adult thing and be understanding. Be his aunt. Be his caregiver.

I waited for a moment, unable to decide what to do.

"No way I'm wiping your ass, Nick," Bad Aunt Laurie said.

His mouth fell open and I could see the panic crossing his face at being stuck on the toilet until his mother showed up in an hour.

"But what I will do," I said, as I stepped forward and created a mound of toilet paper as tall as a Costco-sized creampuff, "is teach you how to do it."

And with a brief but complete demonstration on my part, I showed him a couple of techniques, went over the basics of "Over vs. Under," reached the takeaway of "How You Know You Are Done," and handed him the creampuff.

"You try," I said. "Don't be scared. Nature will tell you in fifteen minutes if you haven't done a good job."

"How?" he asked.

"You'll get a monkey butt," I said, scrunching my eyebrows back at him.

"What's that?" he queried.

"An itchy crack," I replied. "Now let's see what you can

do. You're still skinny enough to do Under, but if you ever reach linebacker size, know that there's another route."

He gave it a shot, opting for Under.

"Give it one more pass," I suggested. "Try an Over this time."

He nodded in approval. "I'm an Over," he agreed.

"Now, look at that!" I said, swinging the flusher knob with my finger. "No one has an open invitation to look at your butt anymore. How does that feel?"

"It feels like I don't have to hold it at school anymore," he replied with glee. "I hate going to the nurse so Grandma can come and pick me up early!"

The boy had reached a milestone—no more cramps at recess—but when my sister, his mother, came home, I ushered her into the living room to talk privately.

"Nicholas asked me something today," I began.

"I did not tell him about Dinosaur Mountain, I swear!" she said, holding her hands up.

"You better not have," I replied. "It took me five months of searching and a bidding war with someone named Freaky Pete on eBay to win that thing. If you breathe a word of it before his birthday, I will tell that kid that I am his real mother."

"I can keep a secret," she insisted. "And he already knows you can't have kids. That you drank so much in college your organs are like pickles."

"Anyway, he called me into the bathroom an hour ago and asked me to wipe his butt," I told her.

"He's *eight*!" we both said in unison, but in very different tones.

We looked at each other.

"Mom has him in the daytime, and you have him at night and on weekends," I began. "And neither one of you thought it was time that he learned this?"

"He's a little boy," my sister argued. "He doesn't have the coordination yet."

I kept looking at her.

"He's not disarming a bomb," I reminded her.

"What if he doesn't do a good job? What if he leaves some behind?" she added.

I continued to look at her.

"Then he'll be more careful next time," I informed her.

"I just don't think he's ready," she finally said. "What kind of mother would I be if I pushed something like that on him and he wasn't mature enough?"

"When is he going to be mature enough?" I asked. "When he has to ask his college roommate to come and wipe him? He doesn't need to understand physics to understand what a white creampuff looks like! And guess what? He's ready!"

"How do you know?" she asked.

"Because he did it," I said. "I even inspected. Your son is now a wiper."

"You mean he asked you to wipe him and you didn't do it?" she balked.

"Yes," I replied. "And now he can finish playing Red Rover at recess instead of being curled up into a little shit ball waiting for Mom to pick him up so he can poop at her house. Don't you dare wipe him! Don't you undo the work I've done!"

It was then that I realized my role in the lives of my nieces and nephews. If my nephew had been so protected for eight years that the kid didn't know the basics of personal hygiene, what else didn't he know about? What other parts of the world were a mystery to him? I could just imagine the shock on his face when he began encountering real life, and how Nick would have gone through a battery of roommates in college had I not intervened.

When he experienced his first tragedy, I knew the day would come in which I would be called upon to guide him with a gentle hand into the world of imperfection and reality.

Several years before, when he entered preschool, the child became consumed and could talk about nothing else. "We have a store at preschool, and I get to be the cash register lady," he told me when I presented him with a new Mickey Mouse game. "This toy is a little boring for me now."

"We get good snacks at preschool," he told me after I made him his favorite, brownies. "They know how to make more than one thing there."

"I don't want to marry you anymore," he told me. "My teacher at preschool is prettier and not so old."

The pinnacle of his experience in preschool came the day he was chosen to be line leader. Handed a red flag for "STOP" and a green flag for "GO," he basked in the glory of heading the expedition of his class from recess back to the classroom without incident.

"You know," he said as he sought out his younger, apparently more attractive teacher afterward, "I've waited my whole life for that."

Then he stopped talking about school, and when prodded would respond simply, "I'm a little busy with the alphabet right now. Can we talk about this some other time?"

Something was wrong. He was hiding something. Then, one Sunday night, he could take it no longer and it all came tumbling out.

Nicholas had made a friend, a culprit whom we'll call "Jim," because that's the name of the bully who bounced a basketball off my head when I was a freshman in high school and left a welt the size of a honeydew melon. Anyway, Nicholas and Jim had spent the entire recess playing together, and when Snack Time arrived, Nicholas asked Jim to sit next to him.

"No," Jim replied cold-bloodedly. "I'm sitting with this boy and NOT YOU."

"My feelings were so hurt," Nicholas revealed to my sister on that Sunday night, after keeping the torment bottled up in his little body. And then he started to cry. This made my sister cry, and when she called me, I started to cry.

It all came back to me. The ringing in my ears for three weeks after my neck snapped back when my head met the basketball. The torture of my entire kindergarten class finding out about my first love, Jay Goldblum, and chanting "Laurie loves Jay!" so relentlessly that I had no choice but to throw up on my desk. The horror of watching my only friend in chorus, a stoner chick named Kay, looking for a piece of gum in my clutch purse after I passed it to her in a motion of trust and faith in our friendship. When her hand emerged, however, it was holding my toothbrush for my newly acquired braces, and she then ran around the crowded choir room with it high above her head, singing, "Guess who has her period? Guess who has her period?" as a renegade maxi pad with an exposed sticky strip flapped around behind it like a flag.

Carrie, despite the pig's blood, had more fun in school than I did. At least she got to be prom queen.

"Who does Jim think he is?" I relayed to my husband later, whose eyes also began to well up after hearing of my nephew's catastrophe. "Nicholas was the LINE LEADER! Do you know what kind of honor that is? He held the lives of his class in his little hands with those red and green flags! Where is this preschool, anyway, in Attica? Who IS this kid, JIM? I'm going to get his address and JIM and I are going to have a little talk!"

My sister, however, handled it differently. She told Nicholas that this experience gave him a good chance to show people how to be nice, and that if he was nice to everybody, the other kids, including JIM, would learn to be nice to each other. It was a blatant lie, but at least it's better than telling the kid the truth, which is, "Little dude, it only gets worse from here."

In fact, I think that children sent out into the jungle by their tribes to survive on their own, armed only with a rock and a loincloth, have a better chance of making it to adulthood than children who live through the terror of middle school.

Things seemed to have smoothed over by the time Nicholas's preschool visiting day rolled around, but I wasn't taking any chances.

"Now, make sure you show me who your friend Jim is," I said to Nicholas as we walked up to the school. "Where does he usually sit? Does he have asthma or any peanut allergies that you know of?"

"Don't listen to Aunt Laurie!" my sister barked as she grabbed my elbow and pulled me back. "Leave the basketball and Reese's Pieces in the car!"

The week after our wiping tutorial, I took Nick to a movie and then I decided that it was time for some life lessons courtesy of Aunt Laurie. I would be damned if he grew up with an abbreviated horizon. There are things eight-year-old boys need to know, because soon they're eleven-year-old boys who think the school nurse just told them they have fallopian tubes, and then they're sixteen-year-old kids who believe that eating chicken and waffles makes them "street," and then they're eighteen-year-old douches pledging a fraternity. And that was not going to happen if I could help it.

"We're going to try a new place for lunch today," I said as I fastened his seatbelt.

"Not Chick-fil-A?" he asked.

"This place is even *better* than Chick-fil-A," I said as I started the car. "Ever heard of a place called Waffle House?"

And there, under the yellow roof of Waffle House, behind the usually dirty windows and the sign out front in the dirtiest window, which says it does not discriminate against pregnancy, my nephew joined the world of Waffle House, where he would see men in tank tops, babies with no parents, and people with fewer teeth than he was born with.

It was a far cry from Chuck E. Cheese's or the wood-fired-pizza place he was used to eating at.

"Waffle House is a place of truth," I told him. "It is a sacred, holy sanctuary where you can come at three in the morning, eat all you can, and then get in a fistfight with another man in a tank top. You can't do that at Chili's. This is the place where you can ask me anything, and I will tell you the truth."

"Wow," Nick said, trying to absorb everything that Waffle House was.

The waitress took our order, then returned a moment later and said, "I'm sorry. Did you want your hash browns scattered, smothered, and covered, or just scattered and smothered? I got menopause. Can't remember a thing."

"What's menopause?" he asked the waitress.

She took a deep breath.

"Freedom," she answered blankly. "Although it makes my wig sweaty."

"Oh," Nick replied. "I'm sorry."

"Sweetie, I've been waiting for this my whole life," she laughed. "I just go back there and wipe my head off and I'm good to go."

"Scattered, covered, and smothered," Nick answered.

After Nick ate what he declared the best waffle he had ever had, I paid at the counter and turned around just in time to see a "traveler" shuffle toward us as we were leaving.

"Hey, buddy," the ragged man asked Nick through an aroma that had taken weeks, if not months, to procure and perfect in equal notes of urine, sweat, booze, and exhaust. "You got any change?"

"I'm sorry, I do not," Nick answered.

"Don't you get an allowance?" the man muttered.

"I spent it on Pokémon," Nick explained. "I don't get very much."

I quickly guided my nephew out to the car and fastened his seatbelt.

"Can I still ask you a question?" he asked.

"Of course. We're still in the parking lot," I replied.

"Was that a bum?" he queried.

"We call them hoboes," I explained. "And that is what happens when you drink too much beer in college after you join a fraternity. You grow up and become a hobo and ask little boys for money."

"Oh," he concluded, "I don't want to be a hobo. He smelled weird."

"That's what you smell like when you live under the freeway," I told him.

"I bet he has monkey butt," Nick added.

"I bet you're right," I confirmed. "You're so smart! I can't wait to give you your birthday present!"

"I know!" he exclaimed gleefully. "Mommy said you got me Dinosaur Mountain!"

"I have a secret to tell you . . ." I said.

Waffle House became our spot, and Nick looked forward to our lunches and breakfasts there. Over the course of a couple of years, he learned what disability checks, ankle-monitoring bracelets, and probation were. Then, when his younger brother, David, was old enough to encounter hoboes and sweaty women in wigs, he joined our Waffle House crew. One of the first things he learned was vital when he ordered bacon.

"Do you want black-people bacon or white-people bacon?" our African American waitress, now completely postmenopausal but still sporting a wig, asked.

David thought for a moment, and then asked, "What's the difference?"

"Black-people bacon is crispy," she explained. "And white-people bacon is soggy."

"Black-people bacon," David replied, and he has ordered it the same way from the same waitress ever since.

Eventually their mother and father joined us in our excursions, and it's somewhat of a tradition to make our trek out there every time I come home to visit. We sat in the same booth at the same Waffle House the day before Kanye West and Kim Kardashian were photographed there, and we are often informed by the hostess or waitress about the goings-on in the establishment that we have narrowly missed by unfortunate timing or because someone couldn't find their cellphone.

"An hour ago, some lady got up and marched behind the counter because she didn't like the way Mark was making her eggs and she started throwing things around," the hostess told David the last time we were there. "And then another woman in a tank top jumped up from a different table and yelled, 'Back off! Back off! I will fight you right here in Waffle House, bitch!'"

"We missed that by an hour?" David, now fifteen, said. "I told you to leave your phone behind, Dad!"

"I'm sorry," my brother-in-law said as we all slowly and sadly shook our heads. "I'm sorry."

You just can't pay for an education like that.

In case some people are worried that I have scarred these children, the exact opposite is true. David holds a 4.5 GPA in high school, has completed ten college courses already, and wants to be a physicist. Nicholas, now twenty, is a double major in an honors program at college. If you ask the kids what I've taught them, David will wait a minute and then say, " 'Don't be an asshole' is probably one of the best. And never to wear a tank top."

Nick, who has had more time under my tutelage, will be quick to answer, "How to wipe my ass."

And what else?

"That Waffle House is a microcosm of society and culture."

And what else?

"That syphilis is making a big comeback, but I do have to add that herpes is far more common."

And what else?

"That you're my real mother, but I'm just about finished with a paper I'm writing on double consciousness and racial prejudice. Can I call you back? Love you."

"Anytime, bub," I reply. "Anytime."

GOY TOY

I looked at the bubbling mass in the vial before me and immediately cast my eyes away.

Don'tlookatit, don'tlookatit, don'tlookatit, I chanted over and over in my head. *And please don't throw up.*

From the other side of the couch, however, the sounds were inescapable. The echo of my husband spitting in his vial hit me in wave after wave, targeting my nausea button and pressing it without mercy.

"Please stop," I begged, after I heard him delivering his deposits two more times. "Or go into another room. Your spitting is making me gag."

"It's just saliva," he countered as I felt my stomach spin like a lazy Susan. "The directions say to get it bubbly. I'm just following them."

"Oh my god," I muttered as I gagged. "You talking just makes it worse."

My vial was close; I only had to drool a third of an inch more into it and I would be done, but I did wonder if the DNA test we were doing this for needed all that spit just to find out who my ancestors were thousands of years ago, or if there was just a little sadism involved.

My husband had been wanting to get both of our DNAs tested for a while after he watched Henry Louis Gates, Jr., use the same test on celebrities and famous athletes for his show on PBS. I wasn't as anxious; both sides of my family are from Italy, and my father is a first-generation Italian American, so I pretty much knew what the results would be: straight-up one hundred percent Italian. My grandfather crossed the Atlantic in the early 1900s at seventeen, although my remaining three grandparents were all born here after their parents had made the crossing, some of them born in Little Italy. My husband's pedigree contained a little more mystery, from the shores of Scotland and Ireland to the marshes of Arkansas, we know there were guns, slaves, a bunch of lumber camps, and probably a whole lot of non-family-values action going on in between.

But the spitting. Ugh. The spitting to give 23andMe, the company we used, enough viscous fluid to test was reprehensible. I finally had to stop and try to focus on my breathing to avoid the eventual hurl that was coming my way. When I got near to the top, I had to stop and seal it.

"That has to be enough," I said. "If they can only go back to my mother with that much spit, that will clear up at least one question."

We sent the spit samples off the next day, and then promptly forgot about them until emails arrived a month later that told us we were ready to have our heritage unfold before us.

My husband went first. He logged on to the website, and within moments, the whole world was laid out in a rainbow of colors.

He gasped. "I'm from . . . everywhere," he said unbelievably. "I am literally *a man of the world*."

And it was true. I don't think there was a continent that didn't have a piece of my husband on it.

"Looking at that," I said sorrowfully. "You could have applied for way better student loans."

"I'm Iberian?" he asked the monitor.

"I thought an Iberian was like a deer," I said. "No offense to your people."

"And West African?" he continued.

"You're from West Africa?" I said. "Oprah is, too! See if she's on your relatives list. Then we can write to her and ask her for money."

"I'm Italian, too!" he cried. "Look!"

"Yeah, yeah, yeah," I pooh-poohed him. "Seven hundredths of a percent. That means you ate macaroni once. Don't jump on my heritage without a wifebeater and an Italian horn around your neck, all right, pally? You didn't even know what an antipasto was until I married you. *Italian*."

"It says right there—" he started.

"Sure. Say '*rrrricotta*,'" I challenged him. "Shut up. You don't even have a nana."

"I'm not Native American," he said, clearly disappointed. "My great-grandmother was supposedly a Cherokee. It says here that I am absolutely not Native American."

"I think that Grandma came from a little farther east," I said, tapping West Africa with my finger. "But now it makes sense that you ordered chitlins that one time. I am sorry I mocked you."

"*Rrrrrrricatta!*" my husband said.

"Please stop. You're embarrassing yourself and the country of Italy shames you," I said. "Now let's look at mine."

I typed in my password.

The world popped up again, but mine wasn't so colorful and was contained to Europe.

"See?" I said, full of bravado. "What did I tell you? All Italian. Nothing but."

"Wait, wait, wait, not so fast," my husband said, leaning in closer to the screen. "Sorry, Ms. Notarrrrro. Looks like you have a little German in there."

I shook my head. "That's a mistake. Absolutely not. German! Do I look blond and blue-eyed to you?"

"Nope," he said. "But your sister sure does."

"Doesn't mean a thing," I snapped. "They clearly brought the wrong baby home, but when they saw how much she tormented me, they kept her out of necessity."

"And look," he added. "There's a little Frenchie in there, too. *Madame.*"

"Stop making things up. It is offensive that you can't accept me as I am," I stated. "I'm all Italian. A little lapsed in my Catholicism—all right, a lot—but Italian nonetheless."

"Maybe you're lapsed," my husband added, moving even closer to the screen, "because you're Jewish?"

I said nothing, almost for a full minute.

"Look," my husband said. "Ashkenazi. Right here. You're Jewish."

"Really?" I said, and leaned in to where he was pointing. "I'm Jewish?"

"Yep," he answered.

"Oy vey," I whispered. "You and me . . . we are one glass eye short of a Sammy Davis, Jr., sandwich!"

Then I took off running.

"What are you doing?" he shouted after me as I ran around, trying to find my phone.

"I'm calling Amy!" I shouted back.

"Which one?" he asked. "Silverman or Segal?"

"Both! I'm going to three-way!" I replied. "Don't you see? It all makes sense now! That's why I always think I am going to die!"

"What?" my husband asked.

I stopped dead in my tracks.

"Dude," I said, throwing my hands up and furrowing my brow. *"I'm in the tribe!"*

"Like this much," he said, barely holding his fingers apart.

"Doesn't matter," I replied. "I'm IN. You can be my Saturday goy."

"What?" he said.

"Well, you're a goy and I'm not, now," I explained. "My friend Cindy told me about this. Her mother has a Saturday goy who does stuff for her on the Sabbath that she is not allowed to do. Like, starting this week, I can't turn lights on, push an elevator button, or even get near the stove. So now those are your Saturday jobs, except that I can't tell you to do it. You have to want to do it for me. Oh my god. I can't wait for Saturday!"

"I don't like where this is going," he said.

"And you're going to need to like getting bagels for me on Saturday, too," I said. "Al Gore used to have to turn the lights on for Joe Lieberman during the campaign."

"So then what do you do on Saturdays?" he asked.

"I don't know," I said. "That's why I need to talk to Amy and Amy. I think I just sit and wait for you to do things for me."

"Well, what do I get from my multicultural heritage?" he asked. "What do I get for being West African?"

"I don't want to be on CNN for not saying the right thing, so that's not going in the book," I advised. "Let's focus on you being an Ibex."

"Iberian," he said.

"If there is such a thing," I muttered to myself.

"There is," he insisted. "They are people of Greek and Roman sources, according to Wikipedia."

"So your people are extinct," I said. "I'm sorry. I can't indulge you in a culture that has died out thousands of years ago, whereas my tribe continues to flourish."

"Some of them are still in Spain," he offered.

"Fine," I gave in. "I'll make you Spanish rice and some sangria. But I only know how to make Spanish rice the Mexican way."

"All right, then," he said, switching back to his profile. "What about my English background?"

"You want beans for breakfast?" I asked. "You got it."

". . . and Irish," he added.

"I'll bake you a potato," I said. "But I will do none of this on Saturday."

"Being that I'm Italian," he said, "maybe I'll make the gravy this Sunday."

"Listen," I advised. "Do you really want to piss off an Italian Jew, brother?"

"You're not allowed to call me that," he said. "That's totally going on CNN."

"Write Oprah now," I said. "If she can't give us money, maybe she can give us tickets to her show, because I'd like a new car."

"Speaking of relations," my husband said slowly. "Did you see this? On your list, there's someone here who shares a lot of your DNA. Like enough for a close relative. I mean a really close relative."

"I told Lisa we were doing this," I said. "Maybe my sister did it, too."

My husband slowly shook his head.

"It's a male," he said.

He looked at me. I looked at him.

"A brother?" he whispered.

"I don't have a brother," I laughed.

He looked at me and raised his eyebrows.

I didn't say anything.

And even though it wasn't Saturday, my goy husband looked at me and said, "Maybe I should turn this off now," and then he shut the computer down.

LAURIE IS A BIG B

"*W*hatcha writing?" I asked my husband, peering over to his side of the bed as I was reading a book.

"Events," he answered as he continued to scribble in his little black book, "of the day."

"Like what?" I questioned.

"Oh, you know," he replied. "Just the usual."

The little black book began showing up at bedtime ever since my father-in-law had started organizing his mother's papers after her death several years earlier. Tucked in among her recipes and family photos, he found her mother's diary, which he transcribed. Then, digging a little further, he found his own mother's diary. It was a little black book that chronicled her life from the time she was sixteen until he was born. Each entry had enough space for two or three lines, merely the events of the day, nothing more, but gave incredible insight into her life at that time. He transcribed that as well, and emailed my husband a copy.

My beloved read through it in a day, and then announced that he, too, would take up the habit. He bought himself a little black notebook, and started documenting his days before we went to sleep that night.

Sometimes he would giggle to himself as he was writing, which I found quite endearing. I would wait for him to tell me what was so funny, but he just continued writing and never said a word. Sometimes he would shake his head, and one time I caught him smirking.

"Whatcha thinking?" I asked, hoping that he would tell me what it was that he was committing to paper.

He shrugged and didn't even look up. "Private thoughts," he said simply.

Private thoughts? *Private thoughts?* What kind of private thoughts? We were married! Were we even allowed to have private thoughts? I thought we shared everything. I thought for a minute. Did I, myself, have private thoughts?

Absolutely not, I determined immediately. I had no secrets! There was nothing I couldn't say to my husband; I was more than willing to share my thoughts. In fact, I am generous with sharing my thoughts!

"Remember I found out that one thing about that one person we know who now does bad things in parks?" I reminded him. "That was private. And I shared it with you."

My husband shook his head. "That's not the same," he said. "That's not a private thought."

"Sure it is," I argued. "It was a secret, which means private, and I thought about it and it made me shudder. That's a private thought."

"No," he said without looking up. "That's gossip."

"That was *not* gossip," I denied. "It is a nugget of disgusting information. And I simply shared it. I felt I was being very unselfish by telling it to you."

"So I could be disgusted, too?" he asked.

"*Yes,*" I replied. "Are you writing about this? Right now? In your diary?"

"Laurie," my husband said, still not looking up, "read your book."

"Remember who told you about every single person in your department that is on Match.com," I snipped. "And that one of the men on your floor is wearing a tank top and licking an ice cream cone."

A couple of nights later, my husband was writing in his journal, and when he moved I caught sight of the page he was writing on. Clear as day, I saw the word "Laurie."

He was writing about me!

"What happened in your day today?" I asked, taking the slow approach.

"Not much," he answered, still scribbling.

"Oh," I said. "You certainly seem to be writing as if a lot happened."

"Not really," he replied.

I sat there for a moment and pretended to be reading my book. I gave him a chance to confess, and counted to thirty before I said, "Are you writing about the dishes?"

"No," he said simply.

"You're not writing about the dishes?" I questioned. "And how I pointed out that you left all of them in the sink this morning?"

He said nothing.

"Without the thought that I shopped for the food, I prepared your meal last night, and that because of leaving the dishes in the sink, I also had to clean up, too, as reflected in the text I sent you this afternoon?" I continued.

He didn't acknowledge me one bit.

"I know it was tersely worded, but as I wrote, if you act like a customer in my house, then I shall treat you like a customer," I added.

He didn't even look up.

"And that I do not think twelve dollars a meal plus twenty percent gratuity is too much to charge you based on the quality of the ingredients and the high level of my cooking skill," I went on.

He didn't even flinch.

I waited for a little bit for him to say something, but he said nothing.

"I know you're writing about the fact that you shouldn't be charged twenty percent gratuity because waitresses don't send you nasty texts at work," I said, going in for the kill. "Because I just saw you wrote 'Laurie'!"

My husband closed the book, put his pen on the nightstand, turned out the light on his side of the bed, and went to sleep.

The next day, as I was taking the sheets off of the bed, I saw my husband's little black book sitting plaintively on his nightstand. I looked at it.

I thought for a moment about opening it and seeing if he wrote that I only deserved a ten percent tip.

I looked at the book some more.

It was right there. All of his private thoughts.

Right there.

Then I pulled the rest of the sheets from the bed and went downstairs to wash them.

That night, as we were lying on freshly laundered sheets, I unmistakably saw him write a capital *B*.

He did not, I thought to myself.

"Did you just write a capital *B*?" I asked.

"Yes, I did," he answered, and kept on writing.

"What was it for?" I asked.

"Are you serious?" he replied.

"A big *B*, right?" I repeated. "You wrote a big *B*?"

"I said yes," he answered. "Why?"

"Because 'Laurie is such a *B*' has a big *B* in it," I stated.

"And I would be writing that because . . . ?" he asked.

"Because today you finally brought the trash cans in, but like I said this morning, you got an *F* for Trash this week," I informed him. "You brought them in four days late."

"Yes, I remember your grading system," he said. "I get docked a grade for every day."

"The trash gets picked up on Thursday," I reminded him. "And today is—"

"Monday," he answered.

"*F*," I said, nodding. "That's an *F*."

"I still don't understand why I get graded every week in Trash," he said.

"As an incentive," I replied.

"An incentive for what?" he said, finally looking at me.

"The satisfaction of a job well done," I commented simply. "And a reward for knowing we are not the laziest people on our street."

"But we are," he reminded me.

"I know," I snapped. "But that's a private thought! No one else has to know that!"

"So you think I wrote 'Laurie is a big *B*' because you gave me an *F*?" he asked.

"I pretty much saw you do it," I confessed. "I have a feeling you write that in there a lot. 'Dear Diary: Laurie is such a *B*. She took a picture of me when she clearly knew my shirt had inched up over my belly.' 'Dear Diary: Laurie is such a *B*. All of my pairs of underwear are pink because she forgot to bleach out the washing machine after she dyed a dress red.' 'Dear Diary: Laurie is such a *B*. She put her hand over my mouth when I was sleeping to make me stop snoring.' "

"You covered my mouth when I was sleeping?" he asked.

" 'Dear Diary: Laurie is such a *B*. One of the cans in the ten cases of Canada Dry Ten that she keeps in the back of the car because she's too lazy to bring them into the house rolled out of the hatchback, hit the ground, and squirted me straight in the eye and almost popped my eyeball out,' " I finished.

"*You covered my mouth when I was sleeping?*" he asked again.

"Only a couple of times," I sighed. "Usually when I pinch you, you stop."

He looked me square in the eye.

"Here," he said, and offered me the little black book. "If you're so obsessed about what I am writing about you, then see for yourself. Here. Take it. Read it. See what I say about you. If you're dying to know, *know*."

I didn't know what to say.

"Take it," he said, pushing it toward me.

"No," I said, giving it back. "I can't. Those are your private thoughts. I have no right to intrude on them even if your underwear is pink, you were blinded by soda, I posted that picture on your Facebook page, and you failed Trash again. And you ate the last of the AmeriCone Dream, I forgot to mention that."

"Please take it," he demanded. "I cannot go through this night after night."

"No," I said again. "That would really make me such a big *B*."

"Fine," he said, and took the book back. I was relieved until he opened it, said "June second," and then proceeded to read each and every one of his diary entries out loud.

It took a very long time. And when he was done, I'd found out that he did mention me; I was not wrong. He read aloud, in three separate entries, "Laurie said she and Amy are having a good time in New York but she fell down in the rain outside of the Yale Club and her belly got wet," "Laurie's neck muscle is getting very developed on the right side," and "Laurie is becoming alarmingly interested in my journal."

"Oh," I said when he was finished. "Was there a big *B*?"

"Yes," he said, and showed me. "Better take in the trash earlier next week."

"Hmmm," I said, seeing it with my own eyes. "Why don't you write about me more? I'll tell you which people in your department are on Tinder."

GOD SAVE THE TWINKIE

The batter, at best, simply looked secular. Its grayish-beige tint reminded me of "Oops" paint on sale at Home Depot, a gallon for five dollars. It was limp, held no body and surely no promise of becoming the sacred item I was hoping it would magically puff up into.

Just like that, the keys to the Twinkie Kingdom had slipped through my fingers and clattered to the floor. I was almost sure I heard them.

Now, I'm sure everyone remembers the Great Twinkie Famine of 2012. It was not an easy time for any of us when Hostess went out of business, which was pretty much the same as saying that someone better build a big boat and start collecting two of every kind of delicious snack, because God Hath Spoken and he was about to do some much needed hosing down of the Earth.

Of course, things change, evolve, move on, companies go out of business. But a world without Woolworth and Hollywood Video is one thing; you can always find flammable pajamas and Nicolas Cage movies somewhere.

Frankly, we have gotten along well without either of those entities and our culture may have even progressed for it. Yes, it is always sad to see staples of the past fall by the wayside, but Revco was an australopithecine and was simply outpaced by Walmart, also an australopithecine, but one that has better connections in China.

But what would the world be without the kind of snack that only the very best of mothers put into their kids' lunches in the seventies? It was no secret as to who was loved and who was not loved when those Dukes of Hazzard and Holly Hobbie lunchbox doors snapped open. The message was loud and clear: "You may become seriously ill or die because you are eating a ham sandwich that hasn't been refrigerated for six hours, but your last moments should be beautiful, so chew on this heavenly Twinkie, should the worst-case scenario present itself."

My lunchboxes typically contained a poisonous deli meat sandwich, a Thermos of milk heated enough by the Arizona sun to be considered runny cheese, and an off-brand collection of cookies called Areos or Neebler, if I was lucky. My family had three kids, a mother who stayed at home and smoked, and a pop-up trailer my father bought to save money on vacations by camping in parking lots near lakes. We were too poor at the time for my mother to slip an individually wrapped sponge cake of love into a meal of possible death and I understood, but that comprehension could not come close to channeling my jealousy, bountiful and fiery, in any healthy direction.

Now, maybe if I had burned out on Twinkies before my brain had fully formed and I developed Section 8 eating habits, I might not be a diabetic today. I said *might not*. My mother will be the first one to tell you that my blood sugar level is not even close to her fault, much like my lady baldness and my deformed kneecaps. Not. Her. Fault. Smoking back then was only *suspected* of causing cancer, there was no solid proof, just as driving around with your baby in your lap was fine until some big mouth said it wasn't and infants started flying through windshields.

And I agree. It wasn't her fault. Had we been able to afford that little luxury, a small, plastic-entombed symbol of her high-fructose love, my priorities may have sprouted in a different direction, like toward the light and not toward the bakery aisle. All I know is that when I started earning a paycheck, Twinkies and spray cheese were on the grocery list for life, and when I wanted either, all I had to do was wash off the Junior Mints cemented to the coins on the bottom of my purse, and I was chewing in seconds flat.

Then came the news in 2012 that the Mayans or Incas, or whatever old extinct ancient people had predicted the end of the world, were basically right in their math. Only thirty or so days short of their mark, the world did indeed come to an end, and suddenly, Twinkies were a black-market item and were going for a hundred bucks a box on eBay.

Hostess, the company that once symbolized the bond between mother and child, was now defunct.

The first week that Twinkies went extinct, I had a dream in which I was racing my friend and fellow author Jen Lancaster for the last Twinkie on earth, and she won.

She's spunkier, and she always has nicer shoes. The next day, after texting her about the dream, she replied simply with an image of herself holding up what was definitely one of the last Twinkies on earth. By my estimates, it cost her $8.33, plus inflated shipping.

I did what we all do in difficult times: bargained, mourned, denied, and then finally accepted. It was not an easy path, but at least I knew I was not alone; two thousand miles away, Jen admired her little golden prize, making the decision every day whether or not to eat it. One day, I knew, Jen would eat her baby. And then she would sob.

I experienced the plague firsthand. It was real. Now, it's not like I ate a box of Twinkies every day, but I had clearly taken the safety net for granted; when I wanted a Twinkie—which might be twice a week, or once a year—it was there.

And when it wasn't, I could hardly stand it. I did degrading things to scratch my itch; I did things that made me shiver with regret moments afterward, and I have to live with that.

I did bad stuff.

And then, after too many dark days, Twinkies came back. A company had swooped in and saved the beloved snack food. It was the Second Coming, and I saw it as the holy thing I understood it to be.

God had changed his mind. The world was worthy after all.

However, I have to be honest here, and I know I'm

looking a resurrection in the mouth, but the truth is, they really don't taste the same.

They don't. They taste a little sawdusty in the cake, and the filling has definitely lost its fluffiness, clearly experiencing a sort of marshmallow prolapse if you will.

I know Twinkies. I could tell when the filling changed in the late nineties from the classic high-fructose magic it was, to a limper, halfhearted imposter. No one believed me, but I knew. *I knew.*

And I also know that when you kill something and bring it back to life, its soul doesn't return. And never will. It will forever be a shadow self.

A Zombie Twinkie.

Sure, it looks like a Twinkie, smells like a Twinkie, and feels like a Twinkie, but the taste of embalmment is undeniable, chalky and dull, merely a shell of what once was and will never be again.

Until a miracle happened.

My friend Kim emailed me a link to one of her favorite shopping sites, and when I clicked on it, two seconds later the clouds parted and the golden light of salvation glowed from my computer.

It was a Twinkie maker. An honest-to-god Twinkie maker for $15.99. Similar to a panini press or a waffle iron, this gadget produced Twinkies in four and a half minutes and, I believe, was the universe's apology for letting Hostess go out of business.

My vision quest had arrived.

Now, I'm sure you think it is completely irrational for

me to think that I could make my own Twinkies. I would say the same. It flies in the face of God. But I have seen it done. There is a small bakery on Eighth Avenue in New York that has mastered the homemade Twinkie. I know from whence I speak, as I have partaken in their remarkable goods. I sat my double-wide ass down at a table and ordered one of everything. A Twinkie. A Ho Ho. A chocolate-covered Twinkie. A red velvet Twinkie. A Sno Ball. From my purse I pulled out a carton of milk and sat there for over an hour, delighted, a pig in red lipstick wearing a Spanx and rolling around in Twinkie mud that was so beautiful I threw all public courtesies aside and chewed with my mouth open while I made a nummy noise. I might have farted. I don't know. I was in a cloud of glory, and in that hour, no other world existed.

So it was possible, I knew, to re-create the alchemy required to produce little golden babies en masse. Babies I could eat without guilt because I could simply pop out some more.

The conjuring began within the hour of the Twinkie maker landing on my doorstep. I ripped the package open, and immediately saw the promise of a new day. The fact that, listed under "Check out some of our other great products," the Personal Corn Dog maker looked unsettlingly similar to the Twinkie maker did not deter me. This was still true when my first try, using the recipe provided in the Twinkie maker booklet, birthed something that looked like a Twinkie but tasted like a corn dog right down to the pig entrail flavor. I had made not Twinkies but Shitties, and fed them to my husband, who remarked,

"You know, I don't see a wiener, but I taste a wiener. If you closed your eyes, you would think you were eating a vegan dog. Same texture. If you found a sightless audience that liked meat cake, this could be big."

My second attempt, a "copycat" recipe found on the Internet, included a box of pound cake mix with some alterations. It was simple, smelled delicious during the four minutes and thirty seconds it took to bring the Twinkie through a full gestation from batter to baby, and, on the first bite, there was no lingering spirit of a processed-meat product. It was not a Shittie, I will admit, but was its marginally less disgusting relative, the Crappie. This was confirmed when I took samples to my next-door neighbor Gemesa, who took one bite and said pointedly, "This is crap. It's so dry I will still be choking on this a year from now."

I am nothing if not tenacious. It took me seven years to get my first book deal, and if I had to spend the rest of my natural existence perfecting the Twinkie, so be it. A friend sent me a recipe that had directions that were similar to launching a rocket into space. First there was cake flour, then there was sifting. Then there was the separation of the eggs and after that it required cooking on the stove to an exact temperature. Then bringing the eggs back together again. Then there was more whisking, beating, folding, and blending. Most people spend less time making a child. At the end of this Twinkie experiment, I had used every bowl in the house, and my kitchen looked like Pablo Escobar had just sneezed on a mountain of cocaine.

But I was closer. They still weren't Twinkies, but when

I brought them to Gemesa again, she nodded her approval and gave me the thumbs-up. When her eight-year-old daughter, Morgan, came into the kitchen, she asked if she could try one.

"Of course," I said. "But I have to warn you that even though they look a lot like Twinkies, they aren't the 'real' thing."

She shrugged and said simply, "What's a Twinkie?"

I shot my accusing eyes over to Gemesa, who could not meet my gaze.

"Oh my god," I said. "Did your little girl just say, '*What* is a Twinkie?'"

"What *is* a Twinkie?" Morgan reiterated.

"I am calling CPS on you!" I said as I pointed to her mother. "I had no idea you were raising your children in a deprivation chamber! Can she come to my house? I have a feeling I need to show her what spray cheese is."

"They just never expressed an interest," Gemesa tried to explain, clearly fumbling.

"What are you putting in their lunches?" I demanded to know. "How are they getting through the day?"

"A sandwich," my poor neighbor admitted. "And . . . an apple."

"And a savory?" I pushed further. "What is it? Doritos? Funyuns? Fritos?"

"The . . . the . . . sandwich is the savory," she barely whispered.

"THE SANDWICH IS NOT THE SAVORY!" I exploded. "The *sandwich* is the *sandwich*. She needs a sweet *and* a savory to round out her meal. How else do you hide your love for her?"

"I made cookies once," Gemesa tried to recover. "I went to Sur la Table in Portland to get the right scoop so they'd be the same size. I drove up there and back in the same night!"

"Take this for your lunch tomorrow, sweetheart," I said as I handed Morgan the fake Twinkie. "For one day, you'll know that someone loves you. And that someone is the lady with the spray cheese and marshmallow fluff in her hair who lives in the dirty house next door."

"It's not that dirty," Morgan replied.

"Your scope of vision is barely thirty inches off the ground, honey, barely beagle height," I said, patting her on the head. "If that's all I saw of my house, I'd think I was a better person, too."

I went back to work in my Twinkie chamber. While I felt that I had come very, very close to the magic I had experienced at the bakery in Manhattan, my quest was not complete. If the last recipe I tried was the closest I got, then that was fine. But I had to try one more time, and without thermometers, sifters, and the folding. Fine if I wanted to make a soufflé, but I didn't need that in my day-to-day survival.

I also posted my attempt on Facebook, eager to let people know that I was going to do my part to make the world a better place. While I was met with lots of encouragement, I also found some naysayers.

"You know they sell them at the store," the movie critic from the newspaper I used to work at commented.

It took all my restraint to not unfriend and block him and then report his comment as harassment or obscenity.

"Yes, Bill," I typed furiously, "I do know that they SELL THEM AT THE STORE. Do you not recall the Great Twinkie Famine of 2012? Do you not? It was a time of desperation and debasement. I shall never return to the creature I was then a-gain."

I complained to my husband that people didn't comprehend my venture and were under the false assumption that history could never repeat itself.

"I can never go back to that," I said simply. "It was a horrible, dark time that I'd really rather forget. The *things* I did. The things!"

"I am with you," he agreed. "I only *heard* what you were doing to that Little Debbie and that was enough for me."

"That's right!" I snapped. "Bring me back to my lowest point when I was nothing but an animal. Do not ever mention that name in this house again. I have my pride back now, you know."

"Please go make some more shitty Twinkies," he said with a sigh and then turned away.

This time, I made a list of all of the pros and cons of each attempt: what worked, what didn't. Did it really need the cream of tartar? (What *is* cream of tartar?) Did the mass egg immersion of the third batch taste too—dare I say it—eggy? Did I want texture more than I wanted flavor? Could I have them both? What I discovered was that I wanted something easy and Twinkie-like, with minimal ingredients.

The fourth attempt was nothing short of a shot in the dark. I got a yellow cake mix, used two eggs to increase density, and then added a half a cup of oil for a softer texture, and a half a cup of water. And voilà. It wasn't an exact match, but it was pretty close. Closer than I had been before, at least. For the filling I simply mixed together one jar of marshmallow fluff, one cup of powdered sugar, four tablespoons of butter, a pinch of salt, and two tablespoons of heavy cream. AND IT WAS PERFECT. As I marched them over across the street to my neighbor Ed's house, I was anticipating a favorable review.

And boy, did I get one. He jumped right onto the plate, popped one in his mouth, then another.

"Oh my god," he said, almost closing his eyes. "Those are *so good*. Oh my god!"

"I know I barged in, but I'm so happy you like them!" I said with joy.

"No worries," he said. "I harvested my pot plant last week and now I'm separating all the buds. It's the dirty work of being a drug lord."

"You're high right now, huh?" I asked, to which he nodded as he chewed. "I hope that doesn't somehow magically confuse the taste of my Twinkie and a real Twinkie."

"Oh, no. No, no," he assured me. "No way. These are incredible. These are *so good*. And I've never had a Twinkie before, so no problem!"

I nodded behind my grimace.

"Are these all for me?" he asked as I handed him the whole plate.

"Yep," I replied. "And expect to see me tomorrow. If

you think those are good, I'm going to blow your mind when you see me write your name in bacon-flavored cheese."

And then it struck me: With a little bit of work and some experimentation, that would make the perfect savory Twinkie filling. I raced back to the house and got my hand mixer out.

NANA'S RECIPES

"**N**icholas just called me," my sister said the moment after I picked up the phone. "You won't believe what he said!"

"I already told him that syphilis was making a huge comeback, so don't blame me," I shot quickly.

"What? No, he was making a frozen pizza in his apartment," she continued. "And he called me with a question, because he said the directions on the box said to preheat the oven to four hundred degrees, but then told him to cook it for fifteen minutes. And he didn't know what to do."

"What do you mean?" I asked.

"He was stuck. He said, 'I don't know how to make this thing. The directions say "cook for fifteen minutes," but the knob only says "bake" or "broil." Not "cook." '"

"This would have never happened if you had girls," I said, shaking my head. "Never."

Now, honestly, I don't care if that's a sexist thing to say; I don't care if it's too gender-specific or stereotypic; it's true. Had my sister had girlfolk, she wouldn't have been laughing at my niece at the same level we were laughing at my nephew now. He's a smart kid. A National Honors student, got a full scholarship to the honors college at his chosen university, and has claimed business and finance as his double major. Still has over a 4.0 GPA. Kid's no dummy.

Except when it comes to survival. And, when I thought about that, it hit me: My two sisters had three sons, three boys none of us had prepared for life outside the womb, who were breathing and speaking and existing due to sheer luck. It wasn't Nick's fault that he didn't know that "cook" and "bake" were the same things, according to Whirlpool and Kenmore.

Had I ever once dragged Nick or my other nephews into the kitchen and said, "Today is the day you learn about our family. Today is the day I pass on to you the legacy that I learned as a child, which you will pass on to your children. Today we are going to make a meatball"?

While my nephews were very interested in eating, they never once showed any interest or curiosity when it came to the regular rotation of meals that were placed before them. And, as a matter of fact, neither had their mother. She will still call me and ask me how to make a chicken cutlet, which in an Italian family is like saying, "How do you open a box of Pop-Tarts?" I don't remember ever learning; I just knew.

Cooking is an important part of an Italian family. We

like to feed people, and if you don't leave my house at least five pounds heavier than when you walked in, that means you did not have a good time and the food sucked as bad as the buffet at a Mormon picnic. There's only one thing you can call an Italian girl who can't cook, and that's a nun. "Go marry Jesus," her family will say. "He doesn't have much of an appetite anymore."

Nana learned to cook at the side of her grandmother, who she went to live with after Nana's mother died of the flu in 1918—"got a fever at ten A.M. and was dead by nightfall," the story goes. She left behind three little girls under the age of three, and my great-grandfather, faced with the reality of placing his three daughters in an orphanage, married his wife's younger sister instead to keep his family intact, and Nana, the baby, went to her mother's mother. She was a little old Italian lady straight off the boat and was most likely no older than I am now, living in a tenement on Avenue C and Second Street in Manhattan. She cooked for the whole family—my great-grandfather lived upstairs—and Nana grew up watching, then helping, and then cooking, mimicking everything her grandmother did, re-creating a little bit of her homeland in her tiny, sweaty kitchen. By the time Nana was married, she was a phenomenal cook, and after she met and married my grandfather, they opened a deli and grocery store in Throgs Neck in the Bronx. She made trays of lasagna and eggplant Parmesan every day, and rolled meatballs into a perfect sphere that I will never conquer. Then World War II came, and the small town they lived in needed to fill the quota of draftees, so my thirty-two-year-old grand-father was called up and told to report within a month. When he responded that there was not enough time to sell his store, the government replied, "If Hitler dropped a bomb on it, you'd lose it then, too." So they gave the store away, and Nana moved closer to her father and went back to cooking for him every day.

Just as Nana's grandmother took care of her, my grand-parents watched my sisters and me every day after school. I would talk to Nana while she cooked, and though she never went step-by-step and told me how to do things, I just picked them up. I watched her dredge eggplant. I watched her assemble lasagna. I helped her roll meatballs. I rarely remember an instance when she or my mother was not cooking; it went on all day at our house, every day. We never ate out in restaurants except for maybe once or twice a year. That meant a lot of time behind the stove for both of them. By the time I moved out of the house, I could make almost anything my mother or Nana made, although I had almost never made any of it. I was not al-lowed near the controls of my mother's kitchen; in fact, I am still not allowed to cook in my mother's kitchen today. On one of my last trips home, I offered to make the Sunday dinner because she wasn't feeling well, and she looked at me as if I had just said, "Can I use your Le Creu-set pots to make some crystal meth? I've only blown up two other kitchens, so I'm really good." The kitchen is my mother's domain, and it goes without saying that I should just consider myself lucky to heat coffee in the microwave in it.

Nana was wary of my cooking skills, too. Sure, I could turn a cutlet over or set a raw meatball in bubbling oil, but when it came to the true magic, I was not even an apprentice. I couldn't even wave the wand. I could watch and observe, but not interfere.

It wasn't until I was in my twenties that I dared present them with food I had made myself. It was eggplant rollatini, and after it was served, my mother watched everyone else take a bite and then sat back, as if she were waiting for the rest of the family to drop dead of sudden-onset salmonella poisoning.

When they didn't, she poked at the eggplant with a tine of her fork, taking about as much as you would give to an infant. I watched her, waiting. Waiting for that face, the face of disappointment, of disgust, of complete failure.

I know that face. The downward curl of her mouth, the scrunching of the nose, the furrowing of the brow. I even have my own version. Instead, she went in for a bigger bite, one you would feed a toddler, and by the end of dinner, not only had she eaten a whole eggplant rollatini, but she was still alive.

My Nana died in 2008, and my mother retired from cooking not long after, and now she pretty much eats out every night with my dad. I can't blame her. She spent every day for about forty years in front of that stove, and now their relationship is over. She still collects Le Creuset pots that I am still not allowed to touch, and the kitchen is still her domain, even if she abandoned it for a booth with fancy napkins and waiters she knows by name.

My two sisters were never particularly interested in being the captain of the kitchen; the younger one, Nick's mom, barely knows where to find milk in a supermarket. My other sister, also the mother of a son, cooks often, but sticks to a Whole30 type of menu that basically means she feeds her family broccoli every night. To Italians, Whole30 is sacrilege; it means that you don't believe in macaroni, bread, and cheese. Basically, she's going to hell.

So that leaves me.

I'm the end of the line.

Now, I've taught my nieces on my husband's side the magic of meatballs, gravy, and pink sauce, and I'm required to make it every time I visit. Again, the boys aren't interested in learning, just eating.

But I think that's going to change.

I've decided that these recipes can't die with me. The next time my nephews ask for penne in pink sauce, they're going to have to roll out a meatball first.

Nana's Sunday Gravy

YIELD: Feeds four Italians, or seven Protestants.

Growing up, we had macaroni and gravy every Sunday for dinner. (For you non–New York Italians, gravy means sauce, and macaroni can mean any pasta. Spaghetti will always be spaghetti. And pasta is actually a word we laugh at and never say. Because it's really called macaroni. I can't prove it, but I do believe the word "pasta" was invented by Olive Garden.) It's an hours-long process, but well worth the wait. To get that deep, rich gravy flavor, the sauce and meat have to simmer together for hours. And hours. And hours. This is the base sauce for all things Italian: macaroni, chicken, eggplant Parmesan, lasagna, and manicotti. This recipe is enough for two pounds of macaroni. You cannot get the same richness from a jar, and it's why there are no Italian vegetarians. It's against our law. Check your DNA like I did. You're not Italian. You might as well become Protestant.

MEATBALLS

2 slices white bread

1 pound nice ground beef

⅓ pound ground pork

½ cup breadcrumbs

1 egg

1 or 2 cloves garlic, minced

½ teaspoon salt and a couple shakes of pepper

¼ cup grated Parmesan or Romano cheese

1 cup olive oil or canola oil

SUPPLEMENTAL MEAT

1 pound country-style boneless pork ribs

3 to 5 Italian sausage links, sweet, spicy, or a
combination

GRAVY

> 3 cloves garlic, very thinly sliced or minced
> One 6-ounce can tomato paste
> One 15-ounce can tomato sauce
> Two 28-ounce cans crushed tomatoes
> 5 to 6 basil leaves, torn
> ½ cup red wine
> ½ teaspoon garlic salt
> 1 bay leaf
> Salt and pepper to taste

1. To make the meatballs, run water over the slices of bread; squeeze it out and place the bread in a large bowl. Add the ground beef, pork, breadcrumbs, egg, minced garlic, salt and pepper, and cheese and mix until well combined.

2. Using your hands, roll out the meatballs; I prefer them to be the size of golf balls, but I have cousins that make them as big as plums. The smaller they are, I've found, the easier they are to manage and have less potential to fall apart while in the gravy.

3. Add the oil to a large skillet and heat over medium heat. Add the meatballs and brown, turning each way until they are browned on all sides. When the meatballs are done (I fry mine pretty dark), remove them from the

pan and set them aside. SAVE THOSE PAN DRIP-
PINGS!!

4. If you are using supplemental meat, cook the pork ribs
and/or sausage links in the same pan over medium heat,
until browned on both sides, about 5 to 7 minutes per
side. Remove the meat from the pan and set aside. Scrape
the bottom of the pan so all of the meaty little goodies
at the bottom are up and floating. Think of them as flavor
nuggets. Using a slotted spoon to keep most of the flavor
nuggets in the pan, drain off some excess oil until you
have half remaining.

5. To make the gravy, pour the remaining oil and little
flavor nuggets from the meatballs and supplemental meats
into a large stockpot. Add the sliced garlic to the oil and
cook on medium-low heat for about a minute, until the
garlic becomes a little bit transparent and just brown
around the edges. Add the tomato paste, stirring for about
a minute, then add the can of tomato sauce. After the can
is empty, fill it halfway with water and add to the pot,
then add the crushed tomatoes, basil, wine, garlic salt,
bay leaf, salt, and pepper. Stir well and add the meatballs.
Toss in the sausage and pork, if using, but make sure to
stab the sausage with a fork once on both sides; otherwise
they will explode in the sauce.

6. Cook the sauce over medium heat for an hour or so,
then reduce the heat to low and simmer for the next 2 to

3 hours. I usually simmer for at least 3 hours, until the pork begins to fall apart. Then you have gravy. Never make gravy in a crockpot. NEVER. That is how you make the Virgin Mary cry.

Sunday Gravy Variations

EASY GRAVY

There are times when I want a lighter, easier gravy, and may not have hours to wait for Sunday gravy to come full circle. This version is completely vegetarian, and has more of a tomato taste to it than a meaty flavor. My mother would kill me if she knew I made this and called it gravy.

> 2 tablespoons olive oil
> 2 cloves garlic, thinly sliced
> One 32-ounce can crushed tomatoes
> 1 onion, whole, peeled
> 6 tablespoons butter
> ¼ cup red wine
> 3 basil leaves, torn into small pieces
> 1 bay leaf
> Salt and pepper to taste

Heat the olive oil and garlic in a saucepan over medium-high heat. When the garlic is just turning translucent, after about a minute, add the crushed tomatoes, whole onion (no, not chopped or minced; leave it whole), butter, wine, basil, bay leaf, and salt and pepper. Reduce to medium heat, cook for 20 minutes, and then reduce to low heat and cook for 40 minutes until the onion is softened. This recipe is also adaptable for Pink Sauce (see below) or for Vodka Sauce (also below).

PINK SAUCE

> 2 parts Nana's Sunday Gravy or Easy Gravy
>   (see above)
> 1 part heavy whipping cream

Simmer the gravy and cream over medium heat for 10 minutes, stirring occasionally, then over low heat for 10 minutes.

VODKA SAUCE

Add 2 ounces of vodka and a sprinkle of crushed red pepper to at least 4 cups of Pink Sauce (see above). Simmer for 10 minutes.

Nana's Chicken Cutlets

YIELD: Feeds an Italian family of two adults and three kids.
Feeds a congregation of Mormons.

When I was little, Nana would serve these cutlets with mashed potatoes and spinach and garlic.

> 1 pound boneless, skinless chicken breasts
> 2 eggs, beaten
> 2 cups seasoned Italian breadcrumbs (or plain
>   breadcrumbs seasoned with ¼ teaspoon salt,
>   ⅛ teaspoon pepper, ¼ tablespoon garlic
>   powder, ½ teaspoon parsley, and ½ cup grated
>   Parmesan cheese)
> 1 cup canola oil

1. In order to get a nice cutlet, Nana would put the chicken breasts in between two pieces of wax paper and beat them with a mallet until they became very big and very thin. I try a simpler approach: I trim all fat and weirdness off the chicken, including membranes and other things that will make me hurl if I think about them for three seconds or longer. (People who serve fatty chicken should be sentenced to a lengthy jail term or at least community service. No one ever wants to bite into a mouthful of chicken fat. NO ONE.) Then I get my best sharpened knife, and because I am right-handed, I place my left hand on top of the chicken breast, palm down, and then

slice a thin layer off the top with the knife in my right hand. I can usually get three thin slices out of each breast, sometimes four.

2. Next, place your beaten eggs in a shallow bowl and your breadcrumbs in another shallow bowl. Now dip your beautiful, clean, weirdness-free chicken breast slice into the eggs and then into the breadcrumbs, coating both sides. Repeat these steps for all the pieces of chicken and set aside.

3. Add the oil to a large skillet and heat over medium-high heat. Cook the chicken slices until golden on both sides, about 7 to 8 minutes per side. Place the cutlets on a rack or a plate lined with paper towels to drain the excess oil.

VARIATION: CHICKEN PARMESAN

Using Nana's Sunday Gravy (page 146) or Easy Gravy (page 150) as a base, spread a thin layer of the gravy over the bottom of a medium-sized baking pan. Add the chicken cutlets, then more gravy on each of the cutlets. Top with shredded mozzarella and sprinkle with some Parmesan. Bake in a 350°F oven for 20 minutes until the cheese is bubbly and just starting to brown.

Nana's Eggplant Parmesan

YIELD: Feeds a family of five from Brooklyn, plus one set of in-laws if you make a side of spaghetti. Otherwise, feeds eight.

This is not a hard dish, but it's a time-consuming one, and as tempting as it is, do not wear new clothes when cooking this. It's messy and oily, but it's delicious and well worth the effort.

Brag on Facebook that you're making Nana's Eggplant Parm. Know that you will become famous for this meal by the evening. Legendary, even. When you pass the frozen eggplant parm on your next trip to Costco, you will point at it and laugh. Feel free to mock. I do.

2 medium eggplants (I prefer longer and thinner
    eggplants because the seeds are less prevalent)
3 eggs, beaten
3 cups all-purpose flour, seasoned with
    ½ teaspoon garlic powder, ¼ teaspoon salt,
    ⅛ teaspoon pepper, and ½ teaspoon parsley
1 cup canola oil
Nana's Sunday Gravy (page 146) or Easy Gravy
    (page 150), at least 3 cups
1 cup grated Parmesan cheese
16 ounces fresh whole-milk mozzarella, shredded

1. Begin by slicing the top off the eggplant and peeling it. (Don't argue. Peel it. By the time you are done peeling

it, parts of it will turn brown. It's okay. Everything is going to be fine. It's not going to rot before your eyes like all of Catherine Deneuve's lovers in *The Hunger*.) Starting at the end you just sliced off, cut each slice thinly and evenly into ¼-inch-thick rounds. Submerge the slices in a bowl of lightly salted lukewarm water. (This draws out the bitterness of the eggplant.) The water will turn brown after several minutes, so when your show is over, retrieve the eggplant, dump the water, and put the slices in a colander.

2. Place the beaten eggs in a shallow bowl and the seasoned flour in another shallow bowl. I like to use an old pie plate for this, so I can shake the eggplant around, and even coat several slices at a time.

3. Heat the oil in a large skillet over medium-high heat. One by one, dip the eggplant slices in the egg and then in the flour. When both sides are floured, fry, baby, fry, 1 to 2 minutes per side until a nice golden color.

4. By the end, yes, your fingers and the fork you use to turn over the eggplant in the pan will be utterly disgusting, but you gotta make a mess before you make something beautiful. Look at what's left over after a baby is born (no, I don't have a recipe for that) or the floor of an artist's studio. You are *creating* here; you are making one of the world's ten best meals in the history of mankind. Revel in it.

5. Place the fried eggplant on a rack or on a plate lined with paper towels and allow to drain. Preheat the oven to 375°F.

6. To assemble the eggplant parm, spread a thick layer of gravy on the bottom of a 9 x 13-inch baking dish. Cover with slices of fried eggplant. Then add another layer of gravy, then a layer of grated Parmesan cheese, then a layer of mozzarella. (May we have a word about mozzarella, please? First, it's not called *"motts-a-rell-ah."* It's pronounced *"mootz-a-dell-eh,"* which is much funner and much less Midwest-sounding than *"motts-a-rell-ah."* Mootzadelleh. Mootzadelleh. Mootzadelleh. Awesome.)

7. So we're going to layer thin slices of mootzadelleh over the Parmesan cheese and gravy, and it doesn't need to be solid. A little here, a little there. It will spread. On your last layer—there will be three—spread the gravy a little more liberally around the top, and then add a heartier amount of cheese, both parm and mootzadelleh.

8. Bake for 15 minutes covered with tinfoil, and then remove the foil and bake for an additional 25 minutes uncovered, until the cheese is bubbly and slightly browned on top.

9. Slice. Serve. Amaze.

Half Nana's, Half Laurie's Lasagna

YIELD: Feeds an immediate family of five Italians, or seven to eight of regular folk.

This is the creamiest, most delicate lasagna in the world. A go-to for funerals. I used to be a snob about ready-to-bake lasagna noodles and only used fresh sheets of it, which I could usually find in the fresh pasta section of a grocery store. Then one day they stopped carrying it at my Safeway and I was at a loss until I degraded myself enough to buy the no-boil pasta sheets on the dry macaroni aisle. Honestly, I actually liked them better—they held a nice consistency that wasn't soggy and made the layering much easier. I released my pasta snobbishness and apologized to the box of noodles.

3 tablespoons butter

4 cloves garlic, crushed with a garlic press or minced

3 tablespoons all-purpose flour

1½ cups milk

¾ teaspoon salt and ⅛ teaspoon pepper (add more to taste)

32 ounces whole-milk ricotta

¼ cup grated Parmesan cheese

16 ounces fresh whole-milk mozzarella, diced into ½-inch cubes

Nana's Sunday Gravy (page 146) or Easy Gravy (page 150), at least 3 cups

16 ounces traditional lasagna noodles (cooked
according to package instructions), or
fresh noodles, or no-boil, ready-to-bake
noodles

1. Preheat the oven to 350°F.

2. First we're going to make a basic roux, which is a simple
white cream sauce. In a large saucepan melt the butter over
medium heat and add half the garlic and cook for 1 minute.
Add the flour and stir until it makes a paste. Add the milk.
Stir well and continue stirring until thick. Add ¼ teaspoon
of the salt and ⅛ teaspoon pepper. It will thicken in several
minutes; keep stirring constantly. When a thickened consistency is reached, remove from the heat.

3. In a large bowl, mix your ricotta, the remaining garlic,
the remaining ½ teaspoon salt, pepper to taste, and the
Parmesan cheese. Add the mozzarella, reserving one third
for the top of the lasagna.

4. Next, spread a thin layer of gravy on the bottom of a
9 x 13-inch baking dish. Place a layer of the lasagna noodles on top. Drop tablespoons of the ricotta mixture in
equal amounts over the first layer. These will even out
with the heat of the oven. Then dot gravy over the cheese
mixture, and drizzle the roux over the gravy. Build another layer with noodles, cheese, gravy, and roux, and another. On the last layer, after spreading the roux, sprinkle

the remaining mozzarella over the top, and sprinkle with Parmesan cheese if you like.

5. Bake, covered with tinfoil, for 40 minutes. Remove the foil and continue to bake for another 20 minutes, until the top begins to brown a little bit. Let the dish sit for 5 minutes before cutting and serving.

Nana's Pizza and Pizza Sauce

YIELD: Makes one pie. This is an afternoon snack for three Italian kids and their Pop Pop.

When we were in elementary school, my grandparents would take us to their house after school and we would stay there until my mother got home from work. On very lucky days, which were almost every other day, Nana would have pizza waiting for us when Pop Pop pulled up with us in the car. It was a Roman-style square pizza, drizzled with olive oil, with a light, crisp crust. It was amazing, and not only is it completely simple to make, the dough rises in one to two hours, and can also be refrigerated for use later in the week. This dough is the basis for Nana's Sausage Bread (page 161), Cold Cut Bread (page 162), and calzone and zeppole.

NANA'S PIZZA SAUCE

 2 tablespoons olive oil
 1 garlic clove, minced
 One 32-ounce can crushed tomatoes
 ½ teaspoon salt

Place the oil in a small saucepan and heat over medium heat. Add the garlic and cook for 1 to 2 minutes until golden. Add the crushed tomatoes and salt, and cook over medium-high heat for 10 minutes, stirring occasionally. Reduce to simmer for 15 to 20 minutes. (You will have enough sauce for two pizzas. You can freeze unused sauce and save until your next pizza night.)

NANA'S PIZZA DOUGH

 2½ teaspoons dry yeast
 1 cup lukewarm water
 1 teaspoon sugar
 2¾ cups all-purpose flour
 1 teaspoon salt
 2 tablespoons olive oil

Combine the yeast, water, and sugar in a small bowl and mix briefly. Let the mixture sit for 10 minutes. Pour the mixture into the bowl of a stand mixer fitted with a dough hook. Add all the remaining ingredients. Mix on medium speed for 3 minutes. Cover with plastic wrap and place in a warm area. Let the dough rise for 1 to 2 hours until doubled in size.

TO MAKE NANA'S PIZZA

> 1 recipe Nana's Pizza Dough
> 2 cups Nana's Pizza Sauce
> ¼ cup grated Parmesan cheese
> 3 ounces provolone cheese, sliced
> 8 ounces fresh whole-milk mozzarella, thinly
>   sliced or shredded

1. Preheat the oven to 400°F. Grease a cookie sheet or jelly roll pan with a light smear of olive oil.

2. Spread the dough out with your hands to fit the cookie sheet, or roll the dough out in the pan if using a jelly roll pan. Make sure the dough stretches into the corners of the sheet or pan. Let the dough sit for 10 minutes. Spread the sauce over the dough and sprinkle with Parmesan. Tear the provolone into bite-sized pieces and place evenly over the sauce. Top with the mozzarella. Bake for 20 to 25 minutes, until the top is bubbly and golden brown. Slice into squares and serve.

Nana's Sausage Bread

YIELD: About 20 slices

When we first moved to Arizona, Nana would always bring her sausage bread to potlucks as we met our new neighbors. Within a matter of weeks, offshoots and pale imitations of her sausage bread began to pop up at these events, and my sisters and I would giggle. They were never as good as Nana's. Not even close. One of the first recipes Nana taught me to make was this bread. The first one I made without her assistance was a wreck. It leaked all over the place and wouldn't stay closed. Sausage bread is comparable to stromboli, but I've never had any version that could come close to comparing to hers, despite the copycats. The dough for this bread is Nana's Pizza Dough. Again, it's a quick-rise bread that is simple to prepare, easy to roll out, and hard to mess up.

> 1 recipe Nana's Pizza Dough (page 159; note that
>   sausage bread uses just half the dough from
>   this recipe, but do *not* halve the recipe; instead,
>   make an extra bread or freeze the extra dough)
> 1 egg, beaten
> ½ cup grated Parmesan cheese
> 2 sweet Italian sausage links

1. Preheat the oven to 400°F. Grease a cookie sheet or jelly roll pan with olive oil.

2. Spread the dough out with your hands to fit the cookie sheet, or roll the dough out in the pan if using a jelly roll pan. Make sure the dough stretches into the corners of the sheet or pan. The dough will be thin. Spread the beaten egg over the entire surface, then sprinkle the Parmesan cheese equally over it as well. Squeeze the sausage from its casing and pinch off bits about ½-inch big. Dot them over the surface until covered. Beginning at one of the long sides of the dough, on the 17-inch side, flip the edge over onto itself by about an inch. Press lightly for a good stick. Then, gently and tightly, continue to roll the dough over on itself until you have reached the other side of the pan and the dough forms a long, smooth tube. Pick it up, place it in the center of the pan, and tuck the ends in. Brush the top of the bread with melted butter, oil, or additional beaten egg. The egg spread on the surface of the rolled-out dough should provide a nice seal, but you can press firmly along the seam to double-check. Bake for 25 to 30 minutes, until golden on the top and bottom. Slice into 1-inch increments.

VARIATION: COLD CUT BREAD

1. This recipe is simply a different version of Nana's Sausage Bread (page 161). The dough and preparation are the same, as is the type of pan to use. The beaten egg is spread over the dough, then the cheese is sprinkled on top. Cover the surface with 9 slices of ham, 12 slices of salami, and 9 slices of provolone. The bread is rolled in the same man-

ner, tightly, from long end to long end, and set in the center of the pan with the ends tucked under. Preheat the oven to 400°F. Bake for 25 to 30 minutes, until golden on the bottom and top. Slice into 1-inch increments.

2. The variations of this bread can include anything; this past Thanksgiving I used prosciutto, capocollo, and fontina; vegetarian options can include sun-dried tomatoes, olives, and artichoke hearts. Bring this to a party or potluck or serve it at dinner, and the next time you arrive at an event, don't be surprised if there's a copycat bread already placed on the table.

MAKE ME A DRESS!!

*T*here was no way the dress was going to fit me. Ever.

And there's rarely anything as sad as finding the perfect dress, in the perfect style, in the perfect fabric, and not being able to get the sleeves on above your elbows. It's almost exactly the same as suddenly finding your soulmate one unexpected day, only to find out he married someone else yesterday.

I just don't get it. If someone would actually step forward and make the same awesome dresses for chunkier girls as they do for skinnier girls, they'd make a fortune. Just because I weigh more than the average college freshman doesn't mean I don't want to wear nice things. I still have to get dressed every day. I still want to wear things I like. I still like fabrics other than polyester or knits with strawberry prints on them.

I was still complaining about this to my husband seven hours later during dinner.

". . . and it's like he said, 'Whoa. I just got married yesterday,' you know?" I whined.

My husband laughed. "I thought your soulmate already got married," he said.

"He did?" I raised my eyebrows. "*When?* I didn't see that on TMZ! He married the baby mama, didn't he? *Goddamnit.*"

"You know, maybe you should take a sewing class," he said. "This way you could pick out the style, the fabric, and you could make it fit you perfectly. You could have any dress you can imagine."

"I can barely make a bed the right way," I said, shaking my head. "I don't think I could make a dress."

"I bet you could," he replied. "You should take a class just to see. If it doesn't work out, then you haven't lost anything. But if you could really make a dress—your problems are solved. Forever."

I realized that he was right. He had actually bought me a sewing machine for our first anniversary, one of the best presents I ever got. I just really didn't know how to use it. So why shouldn't I take a class? After all, when I wanted to learn how to metalsmith, I took a class at a community center and found out it was something I loved, and I was dealing with oxygen-fueled torches there that could cremate an entire class of middle-aged women with one wrong point of the tip.

Amazingly, no one died—no one even needed one single skin graft—although the smell of burning hair wafted about frequently. So why be afraid of sewing? The only person I could really hurt was myself, and even then, sewing your fingers into a hand mitt is nothing that urgent care hasn't seen a million times.

So I found a beginners' class at the same place I took metalsmithing, and I signed up. In two weeks, I was going to learn how to sew.

Still, I was terrified. I had visions of myself walking around the mall in a dress that slowly begins to fall apart—first the sleeves, then the skirt, then the bodice. And then I'd be standing outside of American Eagle in a bra and girdle, almost as naked as the mannequins in the window wearing clothes.

Or what if I made a dress and I thought it was awesome, but everyone else thought it would be a perfect fit for a sister wife? My mother used to sew, and made a lot of our clothes when we were little kids. I decided to get her take on it.

"Oh god," she said immediately. "Why? Why? That's what poor people do!"

"You used to make our clothes," I reminded her.

"Yes!" she said. "Because we were poor! It was the seventies. Gas and sugar were expensive! But TV, that was free then."

"I can't find any clothes I like in my size," I explained. "All the chubby girl clothes are awful."

"Tell me about it," she complained. "I haven't touched a button in fifteen years."

"Do you think I can do it?" I asked.

She scoffed. "If a six-year-old in India can do it, so can you!" she asserted with pride. "But I'm telling you right now, if you start making long skirts and sunbonnets, I'm calling your doctor."

I was still nervous when I showed up to the first class,

and was a little stunned to find out that I was the only person in the class allowed to vote aside from the instructor.

They were children. Not like the kids making clothes for the Gap, but children by American standards. College freshmen and high school girls.

I guess I'm just a late-in-life seamstress, I told myself. I'm the only person in this room who has danced to the original version of "You Spin Me Round." In a gay bar. When I still wore clothes with zippers.

The first class wasn't hard. We learned how to thread a machine, practiced sewing a seam, going backward, and how to change a bobbin. All in all, it really wasn't that difficult, and there wasn't a lot to remember. If you paid attention to what you were doing, you could hardly go wrong.

With that obstacle and the basics under my belt, I learned something even more important at the next class. If you make a dress out of a sheet that you got at Goodwill, as all of my classmates did and thought themselves very clever for doing so, you will end up with a dress that looks like it was made out of a sheet from Goodwill.

Maybe I'm a snob, but if I'm going to spend the time and effort cutting out a pattern, stitching up the pieces, hemming it, and putting buttons/zippers/fasteners on it, it is not going to be with fabric that has even come close to having had contact with the naked flesh of a stranger or any of their body fluids. I looked at the girls wrapping themselves in those disgusting sheets and I wanted to throw up. For all they knew, someone died in them. It happens. My sister sold Nana's bed at a garage sale for fifty bucks with nary a mention that it was where a little old lady drew her last breath, and the bed could feasibly be haunted by a four-foot, eight-inch Italian woman floating above it demanding that someone turn on *Law and Order* and get her a Werther's, immediately. People go to hell for things like that, you know. Those sheets are out there somewhere, too. Someone has them. Someone's sleeping on them or wearing them as a maxi dress. Not gonna be me.

I made my dress from silk, bought at Jo-Ann because I had a forty-percent-off coupon, so that makes up for it a little. I figured if this was going to be a dress I would wear, the fabric had to be important. It had to be something that I liked, and not something that I could have gone to the Women's World section in Target and bought. Because that was the point, wasn't it, to make things I couldn't get anywhere else?

And that's what I kept in mind when I finished my first dress, with a bodice so big I could have breastfed a preschooler in there, which I wore exactly twice, and wore it proudly. My second dress was a little bit better, straighter seams, a cute vintage pattern from the 1950s that I bought and made out of pink lawn fabric with tiny roses on it. I even got a compliment on it. My third dress was made from a 1960s pattern in a stretch Ralph Lauren wool that I picked up online for just three dollars a yard, and I actually added trim to it and beautiful vintage glass buttons.

Every time I made another dress, I learned something else. How to sew French seams, how to slash a facing to make it fit a curve, how to not punch the dress form when I kept on insisting that the facing went on backward. Today, I still remain thankful that the dress form doesn't have hands to call the cops on me.

The thing is, when you realize you can make pretty much anything you want, in whatever color and with arm holes big enough to fit the giant redwoods that sprout from your shoulders, things can get a little out of hand.

When I filled up my first cupboard with fabric, I thought, Wow. I've got enough here to supply me the rest of my life with incredible dresses. But the problem was that manufacturers didn't stop making fabric after that. Even though I had enough, they would make a sueded silk I had to have, or a polka-dotted jacquard that would look awesome as a skirt, or a Liberty lawn, that fabric that was so retro forties that I had to have four yards of it to create a dress.

The overflow from the cupboard went into bins, and it was at this point that I realized that I had a growing problem and a growing collection. The complication is that I'm an expert shopper, I am literally the cheapest person I know, and now that I have figured out where to go and what to buy, you'll never again see me at Jo-Ann with a forty-percent-off coupon in my hand. Once, on a trip to Los Angeles, I wandered into the garment district and ended up at UPS with a friend who had to help me carry fifty pounds of fabric while I prayed that my husband wasn't home when it was delivered. But when you're looking at amazing fabric at three bucks a yard, that's twelve dollars for a dress. *Twelve dollars.* That's cheaper than slave labor, *cheaper*! When you are the slave, the dress is practically free!

So then I had to turn my office closet into storage for the new, wonderful fabrics I found and carted home, or bought online, or, once or twice, found at Goodwill. I have even found, several times, the exact fabrics that my favorite designer uses on eight-hundred-dollar dresses that I could never afford. But that I have made.

And I am not alone. Everyone who has taken up sewing tells the same story. One day, they're making something out of cotton, and the next, a contractor has drawn up plans for an extra fabric room. ROOM. My friend Marjorie had to add a room to her house, almost like she was adopting another child. And as outlandish as that seems, I understand it, and I am so jealous I could spit. When I think of an entire room full of my favorite fabric, I experience a joy so enormous it's as if I'm drinking a Coke Icee through a chocolate Twizzler straw. I might even be wearing candy clothes; I don't know, because the happiness is so completely overwhelming, I am simply dazzled.

Then, one day, I was in Phoenix at a fabric remnant store that is, by far, my favorite place to feed my addiction. They sell mill ends and buy the returned fabrics from many of the online retailers that carry some pretty high-end stuff. Silk chiffon for ninety-nine cents a pound. Liberty lawn for three dollars a yard. (I bought ten. All they had.) With a blue-checked wool that I had just seen in a Prada ad, several bolts of linen for two dollars a yard, and a heap of gorgeous chocolate cotton-stretch velvet, I found myself holding an entire cowhide and trying to determine how many purses I could make out of it. Not only could I make them, my mind raced, I could sell them! On Etsy! At craft fairs! I could make my own website! I could open a store and sell my purses there! I could make wallets out of the scraps, then belts, and then—*oh my god*—I could make shoes!

I COULD MAKE SHOES!

I think I had stopped breathing for a while because when I came up for air, I looked at the dead cow skin in my hands and tossed it back into the bin with a shudder. The other forty yards of fabric came home, naturally, but I couldn't believe I had come so close.

I believed I could make shoes.

Those are the thoughts of an insane person. If any of my friends told me at lunch, "I'm going to make shoes," I would think, Did God tell you not to take your pills again? Because only wizards can make shoes.

But there I was, fully believing it for seconds, because once you can make a dress, there really is very little else to conquer on the planet. It's a very special power, and it tends to make you believe that you can do anything, like jumping a canyon on a motorcycle, or creating a loafer.

Even though my addiction to fabric has become a serious problem, sewing has taught me some valuable things in addition to enabling me with moments of complete madness. I have learned patience, which means I do not have the right to hit, slap, or pinch my dress form, because my mistakes are not her fault. Most of the time. I have learned to work carefully and go slowly, and I have tried to transfer this practice to applying makeup, although I still look like my face hit an airbag when I try my hand at eye shadow. Most important, if there is one mistake, it will ruin the whole dress, and the flaw needs to come out and be reworked, meaning you cannot sew drunk. So that's helpful. Now that I have been sewing for several years, and I make most of my own clothes, I want to create something the right way in order to make it last. There are no beneficial shortcuts when you are constructing something, no matter what you see on *Project Runway*. You don't use glue on a hem. In 1993, sure, I would staple the hem of my dress up on the parts where it might have fallen, but I spent much of my time under the influence of *something,* so much that I might have made a dress out of a urine-soaked Goodwill sheet.

So when a friend asks me across a dinner table, "Did you make that?" and I answer in the affirmative, the second comment is always the same.

"Can you make me a dress?"

I try not to burst out laughing, although I did tell one friend that I liked her way too much to make a dress for her.

"I'll do you one better," I've learned to reply. "I'll tell you where you can take sewing lessons. But stay away from the sheets."

BEHOLD THE POWER
OF CHEESE

"Honey," my husband said, shaking me awake. "Honey, honey. Wake up. The cheese people are on the phone and it's time for you to go."

"Okay, okay," I said reflexively, waking up from a dream in which, standing in a very long line at a fancy bar, I ordered some liqueur that they were out of. So I ordered some wine—a Barbera. Out. An Abruzzo. Out. A Montepulciano. Out. Then I started yelling in something I didn't know I could speak, and the volume of it broke the bartender's head. (He was wearing a gold pumpkin-like mask. Of course.) It fell off in pieces on the bar, and we both started laughing as we tried to put it back on together. "You made me speak my Fury Language!" I said, and then we high-fived.

"Honey," my husband said once more after I momentarily fell back asleep, again, and was spooning Brie into the bartender's mouth. "Wake up. Your cheese class started five minutes ago!"

Don't ask me how I forgot. For the past week, butterflies would flutter in my stomach every single time I thought about the cheese class that upcoming Saturday. I was going to learn how to make cheese. In my mind, that's more pivotal than making a baby or even world peace.

Cheese. Seriously, *cheese*. Cheese is the wizardry of the food world. If you can make cheese, there is really not a higher peak you can reach as a mortal. I'm never going to climb Mount Everest because there's no Cinnabon there; I'm never going to sail around the world because all of the countries are already taken and other discoverers have named them; I'm never going to wingsuit-fly off the Eiger due to fears that Russia might mistake me for a passenger plane and shoot me down; I'm never going to dive into glacial meltwater in Iceland when I can already buy it at the store; and I'm never going to do the Cheryl Strayed thing because I have no current addictions other than toilet paper, and I don't feel that requires working through.

I don't need any of that shit.

I do, however, need to make cheese.

I threw on some clothes, passed on brushing my teeth (I was going to be eating cheese. Why waste the time?), and was in the car before I knew it, heading toward the rest of my life.

Now ten minutes late, I snuck into the class at a local kitchen store and claimed the only seat left—a tight squeeze onto a tall bar chair in between two close flanking neighbors, in the middle of a semicircle that surrounded a large kitchen island with a sink and stovetop. I hate bar chairs, especially the kind that you have to hop onto, because mainly, I'm not a hopper, I'm a plopper. When I see an open seat, the last thing I want to do is to have to take a running start and high-jump into it. I'm not a little person, but I'm not tall, and with the size of my ass, gravity likes to keep me as low to the ground as possible. So it's the safest method for all those involved. The tipping point is not generous—should I raise that load two inches above its natural perch, I could knock planets out of orbit with the force that I'll go down with. And I'm not a "lone tree in the forest" sort of toppler—I'll grasp, reach for, and pull anything I can bring with me: deck chairs, string quartet, and an Astor.

But the chairs were so tightly nestled together that there was no room to even attempt a hop, let alone a high-jump start. Had the chairs been cars, I wouldn't have had enough room to open the door to get in. So I did the only thing I could do, which was sandwich in on one side, lift one leg up onto the seat, and sort of scoot onto the chair. I kept bumping into the girl to the left of me, who made no attempt whatsoever to give me any space, so I scooted and scooted and scooted until I was able to get one whole cheek on the seat, and then attempted to scoot and lift the remaining orb onto it as well, just like a dog who was dragging its dirty ass over the carpet. After ten minutes of butt wiggling and three near misses of the chair toppling over backward—and you know I'd grab and snatch, bringing my nearest classmates with me—I just gave up, left one cheek on the stool and stood on the other foot.

Of my other classmates, I noticed, none were like me. Which is why I suppose they were all on time and had most likely brushed their teeth. But as I looked around, I saw a mother and daughter pair, an older husband and wife, two blond best friends who looked identical, and for a moment I thought the girl to the left of me was a prop, as in a mannequin, completely ignoring my presence and sitting absolutely still. Props like that terrify me, mainly because of an incident at Safeway last summer in which I was walking down the snack aisle with my sister and nephew, who were visiting. At the end of the aisle was a cracker display on a table and a cardboard cutout of a lady smiling, her arms wide open to showcase all of the types of leavened bread. I was happily chatting along with my sister until the cardboard lady came to life and I *think* asked me if I wanted a cracker. I honestly don't know what it was she said, mainly because I was too busy shrieking. Now, I am not sure what triggered such a response. It could have been an episode of PTSD, because several times earlier that week, I was gardening in the front yard when a disembodied voice would say, "Hello!" and I'd scream, only to find a friendly passerby dropping their waving hand and looking horrified. So it could have been that. Or perhaps it was just a trigger reaction to an inanimate object coming to life and offering me a snack, I can't be sure. Even though the cracker did look good, my repeated cries of "I thought you were a dummy! I thought you were a dummy!" caused her to retract her cracker offer and act as if I'd called her a filthy name. I can't help it if she was very good at staying still and pretending to be unalive, but she should expect some *Candid Camera*–worthy reactions when she suddenly springs to life and starts passing out Triscuits.

Regardless, the still life of a girl sitting next to me never expressed any interest in giving me more space or even acknowledging that I was within inches of her. My other neighbor was an old, sagging hippie with a bottom lip hanging so low she could have used it as a drawer. As far as I could tell, from appearances alone, I was clearly the most passionate about the process of cheese making; the second closest was the hippie, though I can guarantee that she'd use dirty pots. I'm sorry, but it must be said. If you're willing to encase yourself in the odor of patchouli, it must be assumed that you're already quite familiar with the stench of mold, decaying earth, and general feculence. If I have to inhale it while I sit next to you for two hours, you bet I'm not going to ignore the fact that you smell like a grave. You do. When you can find your signature scent an aisle away from beets, Rudi's gluten-free bread, and baba ghanouj, own it and just expect feedback.

In front of me, Keith, the cheese teacher and expert, was heating up a gallon of milk to make our first cheese, ricotta. Imagine my surprise when he pronounced it phonetically, as in "*ree-cott-ah.*" I did a double take. Now, of course, I don't expect non-Italian people like my in-laws to pronounce it with an Italian accent, but a cheese guy who says that when he went to Italy to study Italian cheese making he was taught by Italian masters should try giving it a little *oomph.* I'm going to make a fair bet that they were pronouncing it a little differently in the motherland, and while I'm trying very hard to not put too fine a point on it, when someone at Chipotle asks you what kind of tortilla you want, does she say "*tor-tee-ya*" or "*tor-till-a*"?

I know we're attached to Mexico, and I suppose that I should just be happy that people are saying *"ree-cott-ah"* and not "cottage cheese," but if you are teaching people to make something, say it right. If I took a class on how to make duck confit, I'm hoping that when I bragged about it at my husband's next work party, forty people with subscriptions to *Cook's Illustrated* wouldn't come forward to correct me.

But I didn't say anything as Keith repeated it over and over and over again as he heated the milk to 185 degrees, then took the pot off the burner, added one-third cup plus one teaspoon of distilled white vinegar, and stirred it gently for one minute. I didn't say anything as he scooped out the curds into a strainer and everyone around me cooed, "Ooooh! *Ree-cott-ah!*" and I was still silent when little plates with ricotta on flatbread were passed around to taste.

It was good. In fact, it was great. But it wasn't ricotta. It was *"rrrrree-go-the."*

It wasn't until I heard every other person in the cheese class pronounce it *"ree-cott-ah"* as they sampled their little plate of cheese that I decided to take my stand, or else my Fury Language was bound to erupt.

"Keith," I called out in a crisp, clear voice. "How would you use this *rrrrree-go-the* to make *rrrrree-go-the* salada? My mother would flip out if I brought it to our Christmas Eve antipasto. It would be better than bringing her a surprise grandbaby."

He didn't look at me with a puzzled expression, and he understood exactly what I was saying. "You'd need to let it drain a little bit longer, then put a layer of cheese salt down in a form or bowl, add the *ree-cott-ah,* then more salt, another layer, more salt, another layer, more salt. Coat the outside of the cheese with salt as well, wrap it in butter cloth, and put it in the refrigerator for two weeks."

Come on, dude, I thought to myself. I'm giving you an opening here.

Say it. *Say it.*

"Hmmmm," I said. "That's all there is to making *rrrrree-go-the* salada?"

"That's it," he said, nodding.

"For *rrrrree-go-the* salada?" I repeated. "I could start out with this recipe for *rrrrree-go-the*?"

"Sure," he said.

I nodded. I thought about following it up with another Italian word, but really, the only ones I know for sure have a subtext of raunch to them—unless you count the cured meats I know—so in case he had really been to Italy, I kept quiet. I had already been late to class, so I didn't want to be kicked out for throwing some shade on his mom's anatomy.

We moved on to making mascarpone, which was fine—the class, as a whole, only butchered one vowel, so I really couldn't take issue with that. But when we were done with the sample and Keith announced that we were now moving on to mozzarella (*motts-a-rell-ah*), it was time for an extra blood pressure pill.

"*Mootz-a-dell-eh* [mozzarella] has always been a mystery to me," I piped up, trying to seem eager and get a good look as Keith poured whole milk into a stainless steel pot. "If I could put *mootz-a-dell-eh* on everything I ate, the world would be a glorious place."

I saw the hippie next to me take a glance sideways and notice that the girl who wanted to eat cheese on everything could only manage to get half of her ass on the chair seat. Then she spilled her disgusting kombucha drink all over the counter, and if I wasn't so humble, I'd swear I did that with my mind. After all, if these cheese tricks were true and I could go home at that very moment and make *mootz-a-dell-eh*, I was a superhero. And I finally discovered a use for kombucha, other than inciting nausea; it cannot be beat for cleaning up runny cheese and strawberries. Ate it up like it was acid.

For the rest of the class, Keith avoided eye contact with me, and I got the distinct impression that having a native in his class was dulling his shine. Still, even though he couldn't properly say the very names for the magic he was creating, I don't think I could have found anything better to wake me up on a Saturday morning.

After the class was done, some of the students milled about the kitchen supply store where the class was held and bought the equivalent of magic wands and fairy dust: citric acid and a cheese thermometer. The hippie was lost; no surprise there, but when she saw the cheese thermometer in my hand, she asked me where I found it. I led her over to the display, where she gasped and said, with a wrinkled brow, "I'm not going to pay thirty dollars for a thermometer just to make a fancy name for cottage cheese."

I could have killed her. There was a full set of Henckels

knives two feet away or twine I could have piano-wired her neck with, but I didn't think spending the rest of my life in the big house was worth taking the life of a woman who couldn't tell the difference between a lipstick tube and a Playtex tampon. Instead, I simply turned and said, "*Rrrrree-go-the* is not fancy cottage cheese; it is the food of my people—"

"So I heard," she said.

"—just like kale is the food of your people," I continued, adding another cheese thermometer to my basket out of spite. "And if you happen to have noticed that the Kale Wall at Safeway is now gone, you are welcome. An aggressive letter campaign to corporate repeatedly emphasizing the words 'filthy salmonella hands,' 'fondling,' and 'dreadlocks' got that thing down within a week."

She sneered at me and walked away.

"Kombucha is next!" I called after her. "I already have a first draft!"

I wasted no time, and on my way home from the store, I bought a gallon of whole milk and I was all set to begin my life in wizardry.

I smiled as I watched the thermometer climb to 160 degrees, then 170, then 180. I took it off the burner, stirred in the vinegar, and watched the magic happen. I was breathless.

"Oooh, whatcha makin'?" my husband said as he came up behind me and peered into the pot. "Something from cheese class?"

I nodded and smiled, bringing up the slotted spoon that revealed the beginnings of the curds forming.

"Oh, my favorite!" he exclaimed. "Cottage cheese!"

I turned and looked at him, about to burst into a soliloquy of Fury Language when he smiled.

"Just kidding," he said. "I meant *rrrrree-go-the*!"

Ricotta

1 gallon fresh whole milk (do not use organic;
   it is ultra-pasteurized)
1 tablespoon cheese salt (specifically cheese salt,
   because it is not iodized; available at kitchen
   stores, Amazon, etc.)
⅓ cup distilled white vinegar, plus 1 teaspoon

1. Rinse the inside of a nonreactive (stainless steel) pot.

2. Add the milk and salt and stir several times. Cook over medium heat. When the milk rises to 180 degrees (buy the thermometer; it's worth it), take the pot off the burner, add the vinegar, and stir for 1 minute. Curds will form immediately.

3. Then cover the bowl with a dry dishtowel and walk away for 2 to 3 hours. Do not look at it. Do not lift the towel to peek underneath. Do not stir to make sure the magic you are pretty certain you just made is still there. It is still there.

4. Now get a colander, and line it with butter muslin (again, kitchen stores, Amazon, about six dollars). Butter muslin is not called cheesecloth; cheesecloth is much too open with the weave and you'll lose way too many curds by using it. Butter muslin is more tightly woven, but will permit excellent drainage.

5. With a slotted spoon, ladle out the ricotta into the colander, and let it rest for about 2 hours; less time will provide a creamier ricotta, and longer will make it drier.

6. Add salt to taste after draining. The ricotta lasts up to 7 days in the fridge in a sealed container.

Queso Fresco

1. Exact same recipe as ricotta, except use 2 tablespoons of cheese salt and ⅔ cup distilled white vinegar to produce larger curds.

2. After draining, wrap the queso fresco in butter muslin and weight it down with a can of vegetables or something substantial. Let it drain for 2 hours. The drained cheese will be more compact and denser than ricotta.

Incredibly Easy Goat Cheese

This requires no cooking whatsoever. You only need to locate a large tub of goat yogurt (think Trader Joe's, Whole Foods) and pour it into a colander lined with butter muslin. Drain the goat yogurt for 18 to 24 hours. (You can drain it on the counter if the kitchen isn't very warm, or you can do it in the refrigerator, which will take about 6 hours longer.) And then that's it. Add salt, herbs, honey, whatever you feel like adding. I made a fantastic log with marjoram, garlic, and chervil, and another with Italian herbs that was equally awesome.

Incredibly Easy Cream Cheese

Same method as the goat cheese, except use regular dairy yogurt with the highest fat content you can find. Line the colander with butter muslin, add the yogurt, and drain for 18 to 24 hours. Add salt to taste. I added caramelized onions, truffle salt, and parsley to mine. Take this to parties, tell them you made it, and you'll have cheese cred for life, my friend.

SMOKIN' HOT

*T*he moment I pulled into my driveway, there was no ignoring the smell.

This was truly awful, permeating and sharp, and decidedly not the aroma of spoiled, rotten cabbage that was produced by the paper mill and hung over our little stinky town.

Great, I thought to myself, sighing deeply, attributing the stench to the newly opened barbecue place behind my house that had set up an enormous smoker in the parking lot that piped the same amount of smoke into my backyard as the Polar Express.

"This will not do," I mumbled to myself as I grabbed my purse and wished again that one of my sisters had married a lawyer. I headed toward the front door, where the stink only got stronger.

"I will not live under a rotten meat cloud, BBQ King!" I yelled loudly as I pulled out my keys. "I will see you in court as soon as I make friends with George Clooney's wife!"

But when I opened the front door I was enveloped by a

thickly hanging bank of fog that was accompanied by a burning, acrid stench. It hovered in front of me, so thick it was difficult to see through.

The house was on fire.

Oh my god, I realized, my husband always said this would happen! He always insisted that the two prior years of mail that had piled up in my office would combust before I got the shredder fixed.

The first thing I did was grab Maeby, my dog, and push her outside to safety. After that, I froze. Should I grab the shoes I just got on eBay or the portrait of my grandfather as a little boy? What about the green vintage coat I just found in my size? IN MY SIZE? My sewing machine! Get the sewing machine! TiVo! TiVo! There's a Tom Hiddleston movie on there that I haven't watched yet! How hard would it be to drag my 1948 O'Keefe & Merritt stove outside? I just got awesome Kate Spade tights at T.J.Maxx for $3.99! Those *must* be saved! What about my computer? I'm in the middle of writing this book!

I almost hit myself in the face.

Who cares about the frigging book? I have made what I consider wise investments. I don't have a 401(k). Instead I have a comprehensive, world-class collection of Spanx, which was now in danger of melting into a giant, unusable puddle! At a hundred bucks a pop and enough pairs to rotate before I am forced to do laundry, I have a Toyota's worth of flesh-colored spandex in my middle drawer.

The panic was paralyzing. I didn't know what to grab first. I finally pushed myself to run to the stairs and save my body shapers, keeping my eyes out for flames and falling timbers. While I agree it may be foolish to sacrifice one's life to rescue rubber lingerie, the importance of a well-fitting girdle cannot be overstated. There are those that roll up and create something akin to a Speedo, like two hot-dog-sized tubes on either side of your hinterlands, as they simultaneously cut off circulation to lower extremities and create a pins-and-needles sensation where no one wants a pins-and-needles sensation except E. L. James. There are those that roll downward until they are cradling your fat roll like a hammock rocking a one-eyed, limbless baby. There are those that are too efficiently clingy, enough to cause Spanx Thumb, a repetitive-motion injury incurred by struggling to pull them down in the event of a middle-aged lady coughing, sneezing, getting out of bed, or being told a joke far too saucy for her easy-release bladder. And then there are those that aren't up to the job and blow themselves out on the tenth outing, creating a back access panel where there shouldn't be. Unless, of course, you are E. L. James and need to find another fifty shades of shame.

The closer I got to the kitchen, the thicker the haze was, and as I passed my prize stove, which was now black with char, I saw smoke billowing out of it like there were a thousand tiny little vapers sitting inside, but without the accompanying aroma of candy corn or drag queen.

And because I have watched numerous movies in which people open doors to rooms and cause back drafts that char them worse than anything served at Sizzler, I pulled the door to the oven down and was smacked with a pyroclastic flow of choking smoke and ash. Inside was a giant, broiling ashtray, but thankfully no flames. Just two cookie pans full of what looked like hardened lava, chicken that had changed form from a solid to liquid and became a bubbling mass of charcoal.

This is impossible, I thought to myself. I turned the stove off before I left. I know I turned it off. I had started making my sweet little dog her chicken jerky treats after China was caught, essentially, melting Tupperware into the shape of dog bones and then shipping them to Costco. So I do it myself now, and had just finished the last tray, and had turned the oven off but left the trays of chicken in the oven to let them finish jerky-ing.

I looked at the dial on the stove, still puzzled as to what had happened.

Apparently, it's easy for anyone to think that they are turning the oven off by turning the knob to the right, but they have actually turned it to broil—before leaving to get their roots done.

For a little over three hours.

Righty-tighty, lefty-loosey, right? Right?

Isn't that the law?

Right is OFF.

Left is ON.

Except the law is broken on my stove, and as I just checked, also on my kitchen faucet, bathtub, outdoor spigot, and essentially every other place in my house that defies the law of a well-established and culturally essential nursery rhyme.

So anyway.

I aired the house out as best as I could, employing every

fan I had pointed at open doorways and windows. The smoke, eventually, sort of, cleared out.

What remained was the aroma of a chicken that I had not only broiled but also cremated in my oven. In fact, I did more than cremate the chicken, I Pompeii'd the chicken to the point that if I had the wherewithal to pour plaster over the cookie sheets, I would have had a tourist attraction on my hands.

It did not smell like a campfire. It did not smell like barbecue. It did not smell like jerky. The stink that permeated every inch of my house—every surface, including rugs, furniture, linen, and clothes—was a concentrated, boiled-down, aromatic stew of hot metal and charred meat, accented by notes of burned hair, which all added up to one gigantic death fart.

I quickly Googled products that eliminated "smoke" smell and ran to Home Depot and Auto Express to secure them, hoping to erase the stench before my husband came home. I even ordered dry chem sponges that are used by professional crews for fire cleanup. Despite the effort of spraying two cans of smoke and odor eliminator, and sprinkling baking soda on everything, I heard the "stink" laugh at me as my husband walked through the door at six o'clock, gasped, and then covered his mouth.

"What the hell happened?" he said in between coughs.

"Oh, that smell?" I said, trying to be casual. "I think BBQ King got slammed at lunch today."

"Oh really?" my husband said. "Are they cremating corpses now? Because that is not pulled pork."

"There was an incident," I relented.

"What's all of this white stuff? Please tell me it's house dandruff and that you weren't trying to make crystal meth."

"There was a situation with the oven," I tried to explain. "That oven is NOT righty-tighty!"

My husband's face was beginning to form a grimace. "It smells like a new car in here," he said. "With a Molotov cocktail burning inside of it."

"Did you know that every single on and off knob we have in this house is defective?" I stuttered.

"It's all of that junk mail from Discover Card and American Express, isn't it?" he said, untucking his shirt and trying to use the hem as a mask. "I can't believe you finally set the house on fire."

"I *did not* set the house on fire," I protested. "I only cooked a chicken until it became an element."

"For how long?" my husband said. "Are you still cooking it?"

"No!" I said adamantly. "I got it out before the pan turned liquid."

"Didn't you smell it? Didn't you see it? I can barely see my hand. It looks like China in here!"

What he didn't know was that I had already cleared out ninety percent of the smoke due to my plan of action and that, in my eyes, it looked pretty damn good now. In fact my eyes hardly stung anymore.

"I can't even smell it now," I lied, since the stench had burned itself into my nostrils to such an extent that I knew I would die smelling it.

"Fix it, Laurie," he said.

"I will, I will," I said, terrified to hear what he would have to say once he smelled our dog, who had been marinating in the smoke with her head under a chair until I came home.

He wrinkled his nose as soon as he let her in. "Oh my god!" he snapped at her, as he foolishly attempted to fan the remaining smoke outside with the palm of his hand. "She smells like my grandma's perm!"

"I'm sorry," I pleaded.

"Just fix it," he demanded, to which I simply nodded.

In the days to come, I found out just how evil smoke from a cinder chicken can be. It got into everything— *everything.* And once the smoke settled, a thin layer of black ash covered everything, making the effort of my last dusting, three months prior, entirely worthless.

The washing machine ran for a week straight. I rented a steam cleaner to get the soot out of the rugs. Then things took another turn for the worse when I washed every wall down with water and vinegar to neutralize the smell, and then had to try to figure out how to stop my house from smelling like a torched side salad.

Everyone who came near my house was invited in for a test smell. Neighbors, friends, mailmen, the UPS guy, my plumber, the landscaper, and anyone else I could get my hands on.

"I know it smells like sin and atheism in here to you," I told the young men in white shirts and black ties who were looking to recapture my ex-Mormon husband in an LDS trap. "But aside from that, can you rate its pungency on a scale from one to ten?"

After three weeks, the smell had subsided somewhat but was still very much living with us. The sponges never arrived, and I was encouraged by friends to call my insurance company to report the damage and have the house blasted with oxygen, but the thought of cleaning up so that strangers could come in was just exhausting. As was listening to my State Farm guy say that it was nice to hear from me, but no, I could not collect damages after hoboes had broken off branches in my backyard so they could make a den in my bushes in which to sleep, and no, we couldn't collect damages after my husband got sprayed in the eye by a dented can of Canada Dry when it fell out of my car and no, I couldn't collect damages from someone breaking into my car if all they did was rifle through the maxi pads in my glove compartment, and that maybe I should learn exactly how the F my oven turned off.

So what option did I have?

I trudged down to the basement and rooted around until I found the cans of paint I had purchased ten years before when we bought the house and I had visions of painting all of its rooms, which well exceeded my level of vigor. I had succeeded in painting one room before I got bored, and it still bears an inch-long scar at the top of the wall that shouts the original color and just how lazy one woman is that she *couldn't go the extra inch*. As a result, various shades of fermenting gallons of Restoration Hardware paint had become rusted shut with antiquity and abandonment. With a hammer and a screwdriver, I cracked open the lid of one can, like an Egyptian tomb, and took my punishment.

For the next eight days, I attempted to paint the dining room, which had gotten the biggest deposit of pollution. My walls became silver sage, eliminating the diabetic-urine yellow that I had made myself live with for a decade, and then I decided to paint the century-old crown molding black, adding years to my sentence for bad behavior. It was going to look and smell great, I assured myself.

If I have any advice to impart, it's that you should never paint anything black unless you already have black walls, and a black floor, and a black ceiling, because you will spend the rest of your life scraping tiny black dots off of everything with your splintered, calcium-deficient nails.

You will also spend the next week attempting to get the dark, stubborn paint off of your hands, and will finally give up, happy to let it reabsorb into your body. Although when your new doctor asks you what you do for a living and you answer that you're a writer, she may very well inquire if that's why your hands are all black.

And because the last writer to have ink-stained hands was Charles Dickens, you should immediately put your quill down and find a new doctor, because the one you have is a little behind the times and might attempt to leech you.

I finally finished the dining room the morning that my sister and her family were due to arrive for a visit. I pulled the masking tape off, put the ladder away, and reassembled the room, hoping that I had finally conquered the enemy and that the stink was finally gone.

When I met her at the airport, she greeted me with something of a dirty look.

"I suppose the dry chem sponges that came to my house were for you," she said. "They weigh about five pounds apiece and pushed me over my luggage weight limit! You're the only one weird enough to buy something like that. I saw two episodes of *Breaking Bad* and your hands are black. You're not making meth, are you?"

I had ordered the sponges on my sister's Amazon account (why pay for Prime?!), and they had mistakenly been sent to her address.

"There was an incident, but thank you for bringing the sponges," I explained, not wanting to tell her about the smoke so that she could be my perfect guinea pig. She would be the one to tell me exactly how fresh and paint-y my house now smelled because of all of my effort.

Once home, I swung the door wide open and eagerly waited for the verdict.

"God," she said as she wrinkled up her nose the minute she stepped into my house, and then she looked at me with her Level One face. "*Why does your house smell like the permed heads of ten Nanas?*"

FATTY FATTY
TWO BY FOUR

"All righty," my doctor said as he entered the examination room. "How are you, Miss Ontaro?"

I hate going to the doctor. It takes a lot to get me to go, like a scissor sticking up out of my foot, a kidney stone that threatens to shoot out of a major organ and right through the skin, or something the size of a tennis ball attempting to colonize my neck.

"Oh, you know," I said, obviously. "Could be better."

"I see, I see," he nodded, and honestly, I hate that. Because this particular doctor has never cured me of anything. Never. I'm usually better on my own in the dim light of my filthy bathroom, dousing whatever ailing part of me with my version of first aid, which consists of hydrogen peroxide, three Benadryls, and a Valium. Covers all bases, and I'm usually good to go in forty-eight hours, depending on how expired the Benadryl is.

But this time, I couldn't treat myself. I had tried and failed, and, at my husband's insistence, finally made an appointment with my primary care physician, whom I have no faith in whatsoever. As I've reported before, his first questions are a) how my poop was that morning; b) do I jog; and c) has he ever given me the recipe for his bran muffins.

Seriously. This is all he knows about medicine, and there are times when I am more likely to trust the primitive advice of some of my distant relatives to put a poultice of toothpaste and Vaseline on every ailment. It has cured cancer and arthritis, but is sadly ineffective on alcoholism and drug manufacturing in one's trailer. This guy's no better. I believe he holds about as much curative power in his hands as the girl at Taco Bell who just made my burrito and had a tattoo of Hello Kitty sprawled across her neck, and one of those people only charges me eighty-nine cents.

This utter lack of faith was confirmed one day when I was driving to Safeway and I saw a skinny man jogging, wearing tiny blue satin shorts riding so far up his ass it looked like a set of flappy butt boobs. In my rearview mirror I recognized him as the man who had recently told me that bran muffins would benefit my suspected toe fungus.

So now I was in his office by force, and he looked at me and said, "Whatcha got going on there, huh?" referring to the brace on my left hand.

"Oh, no," I replied. "I'm not here for that. I have a sinus infection from a leftover cold and my ears are clogged up. And now I'm having a bit of vertigo."

"Well, what's wrong with your hand?" he asked.

"Nothing really," I said. "But if I could get something to clear up this sinus infection, that would be great."

"Sure, sure," he answered. "How long have you had it in a brace?"

I sighed. "I don't know. A week, week and a half."

"And it's not getting better?"

"Well," I said hesitantly. "I keep hurting it. It's nothing. I don't mind the brace. But right now, the room is spinning as if it was ladies' night, and I was the only lady at the bar."

"How do you keep injuring it?" he asked, and I finally realized that I wasn't going to get him to address my real problem unless I shook him off the trail of my perceived problem.

"It's just a repetitive motion injury," I finally said.

"Play videogames?" he said. "I see lots of that."

I sighed. "No," I replied. "It's Spanx Thumb."

He looked at me and paused.

"How often are you spanking your children?" he queried warily.

"I don't have children," I said impatiently. "Spanx. Bodywear."

He looked at me blankly.

"It's a shaper," I tried to explain. "You know, like a spandex shorts kind of thing, it squeezes you in and smooths you out. . . ."

He still kept looking at me.

"It's a girdle," I simply said. "I have Girdle Thumb."

"Is that slang for shooting up drugs?" he asked.

"No it is not," I responded flatly. "I have injured my thumb by repeatedly pulling up my girdle. As you can see, I'm chunky. Sometimes I have to really struggle a bit to get it on. I've had to take breaks before. It's . . . a process. But if I could get a Z-Pak for my sinuses, that would be awesome."

"Yep," he said, and then slapped his knees. "I'm going to have Debbie come in next."

"Okay," I said, thinking, Who is Debbie? Will she give me the prescription? He didn't even examine me, but I am completely fine with that. So he walked out, and I waited for Debbie.

For a long time.

I was about to get up, go home, and pour alcohol in my ears when the door opened and Debbie finally came in. Wearing perky medical office scrubs with cupcakes all over them. I was ready for her to hand over the prescription so I could be on my way, but instead, she sat down at the computer, looked at me, and said (and I quote): "Are you familiar with My Fitness Pal?"

"I don't know," I said, stumped. "Do you jog with the doctor?"

"No," she said. "The website. My Fitness Pal, the website."

"Um, yeah," I replied, now very puzzled. "It's the place where you log everything you eat."

"It's not only that," she informed me. "It can keep track of your exercise, and help you to be informed to make responsible choices."

I was really hoping that the responsible choices she was

talking about were to not pay one credit card with another, or call the IRS back when they asked me to, or not
honk at a hobo who has Charlie Manson eyes and who
stops in front of my car to have a conversation with a
piece of smashed gum on the ground.

Those kinds of responsible choices.

"See, if you use My Fitness Pal, and that's 'W, W, W,
dot My Fitness Pal dot com,'" she said, spelling it out as if
I were in preschool, "you can trend and track your calories every day, and you can rein in your daily consump-
tion."

"That is awesome," I said, trying to rein in the compul-
sion to kill her, all 112 pounds, size four of her. "But what
does that have to do with my sinus infection?"

She looked at me as if I had just reached into my purse,
brought out an Italian sub, and tore a chunk out of it with
my gnashing teeth. And grunted.

"The doctor suggested I show you this tool for weight
management since I have just lost a significant amount of
weight by using 'W, W, W, dot My Fitness Pal dot com,'"
she said. "Since I've made the journey myself, he felt it
might help you reach some goals."

"Aha," I said, and then I just stared at her.

So. The Fat Talk. We were having the Fat Talk. But
since my doctor was too chickenshit to call me fat to my
face, he sent in his formerly fat nurse to break the news to
me that I was chubby, maybe to soften the blow a little,
maybe to rub it in that someone else had more willpower
than I did.

This man, with floppy blue satin tits for an ass, saw fit

that I should be informed, as if I didn't know. My Girdle Thumb was enough of an indication to me that I had bought a ticket on the Fat Bus, but I also know it's never too late to get off.

As I sat there, looking at Debbie as she showed me her own account on www.myfitnesspal.com and what she ate yesterday, I was wrapped in the unbearable heat of humiliation, and if I could have gotten up and run out of there, I would have. But I had already been charged for the co-pay, and I'd be damned if I was going to leave that place without a prescription for something in my hand.

Guess what? I know what I look like. I know it. I knew it when I went through TSA security in Mesa, Arizona, and, as always, I set off the body scanner.

"Do you have metal in this leg, ma'am?" they always ask me. "Do you have a metal hip? Female assist!"

This happens to me every single time at the airport. I get the patdown. But on one particular day, the female agent who was conducting it was very concerned about my abdomen and kept returning there, as well as swiping her hands in between my legs.

"What is in there?" she asked me. "What do you have there?"

"Nothing," I insisted, and I was telling the truth. My pockets were empty. I had no bomb putty strapped to my waist. There were no firecrackers in my cookie. But when she insisted I did and went back in for another round, I snapped.

It's completely fair to say I lost my shit.

"It's fat," I told her. "You are touching my fat."

"What's this?" she said, running her hands over my belly again.

"I AM FAT," I said louder. "THAT IS FAT."

Her hands went again to my inner thighs.

"CAN YOU NOT TELL I AM FAT?" I said, almost yelling at this point. But it wasn't almost. I was yelling, and people were turning their heads.

"I am telling you it is fat," I said, now in a rage. "And no matter how much you touch me, it is never going to stop being FAT."

She finally stopped assaulting me and let me go, and it took everything I had not to turn around and hiss, "But I have a pipe bomb up my ass!"

The last time I went through TSA just a couple of months ago, I set off the body scanner again, and the conversation went like this:

TSA LADY: I have to touch your upper inner left thigh. It will be a light touch. Do you have any metal in that leg?

ME: No, but you always want to check that leg and you always ask if I have metal in it. I do believe it is fatter than the other leg.

TSA LADY: Oh. Are you wearing foundations?

ME: Certainly. I'm a lady.

TSA LADY: I bet it's bunched up around your leg. That always sets off the alarm. All of the bunching.

ME: It IS bunched up around my leg! I can barely
feel the left one anymore!

TSA LADY: (Extends hand toward my crotch, then
the patdown) Oh, it's really bunched up down
there. Yep, that's it. Mystery solved.

So yeah. Maybe My Fitness Pal helped Debbie avoid
future embarrassments like that, or maybe Debbie got to
third base with her female assist at TSA and it caused her
to join a website and count her terribly responsible calories, I don't know.

What I do know is that when I asked Debbie how much
weight she had lost, to understand her journey more completely, her honesty was more than I was prepared for.

"Oh," she said as she nodded. "A lot."

"Really?" I said. "That's great. Congratulations!"

"Thank you," she said, beaming. "I feel like a whole
new person. I lost ten pounds. That is the equivalent of
two gallons of milk."

"Wow," I said as I nodded back. Ten pounds. Way to
go, Debbie! That is amazing. That you went from a size
six to a size four. Slow clap for you, Miss XS! After ten
more pounds, you can become a medical skeleton.

"I got to buy all new clothes!" she added. "I had to.
One pair of my skinny jeans basically fell off!"

So, this is also what I know: I am not, in any way, im-
pressed by ten pounds. At all. In the course of my lifetime,
I have lost roughly two hundred pounds, and I'm not
alone. Most of my friends could say the very same thing.

We are experts at losing weight. We are the authorities on counting carbs, counting calories, estimating the carb/protein ratio of every meal, not eating after six P.M., pooping our pants with Alli, speeding our asses off with Dexatrim and Diet Cokes for every meal, eating salads with vinegar, and walking the equivalent of the Oregon Trail on our treadmills.

We have done it all.

And if anyone, including my doctor, wants me to lose some poundage, sending in a thin girl who has always been thin but just lost ten pounds to look better in her thong is not the way to do it. If you've never been fat, if you've never lost forty pounds only to gain it back the minute you eat a sandwich, you need to keep your speedy metabolism and your rice cakes to yourself, little miss, because I can squish you like a bug. You're a newborn in the world of weight loss, a poseur, a fraud. Bragging about losing ten pounds doesn't make you an expert. It just makes you laughable.

I know you just see a fat girl sitting next to you, I wanted to say so badly. One that rolls around in a trough of Twinkies like it was a bed of money, just randomly biting at them for every meal. That is what you think I am. So think it. I am past caring. What I do know is that if I were sent to a Korean prison camp (the bad Korea, not the good one), I would be the last one standing, and I would outlive you. Not because I'm strong or because I have an unbreakable will to survive, but because I have a metabolism that moves slower than an old lady paying for groceries with money from her change purse. My body can work miracles; it can turn water into Karo syrup, it can render a RyKrisp cracker into a double-decker German chocolate cake that takes up residence on an upper arm and refuses to be evicted.

As a result, I am a gold-medal winner in the Fatty Olympics, reigning over events such as Stair Spanx, in which a chunk takes to the stairs with Spanx wrapped around her knees because she forgot she was wearing cowboy boots and was too lazy to either yank the boots off or the Spanx back up; Skin Pull, in which a chubby attempts to put on a pair of Spanx without fully drying off from the shower first, or in tropical conditions; Toe Grab, in which something valuable is dropped to the floor and the item can be more easily retrieved by grasping it with the phalanges than in an attempt to bend over; and the most demanding, Floor Rise, in which the athlete starts from a position of sitting on the floor and stands upright without the aid of rolling toward the nearest piece of furniture and using it as leverage.

I am a superior competitor in all of these categories. I will happily challenge Debbie, my doctor, and any naysayer to any of the above events. I will race you down the hall right now with Spanx around my ankles. And *I will win*. I will reign supreme, although my injury from my latest Skin Pull event might take a little while to heal.

"Well, thanks for the advice," I said to Debbie, forgoing the antibiotic prescription because I was done being humiliated.

She looked surprised as I gathered my purse and coat

and stood up—on my own—and opened the exam room door to walk out.

"Oh, but here's a little advice for you," I said, and turned before I crossed the threshold. "Make sure you keep your fat clothes."

MODERN HOUSECRAFT

*I*t was a cute 1920s red-brick bungalow with a fireplace in the living room and a swinging door in the kitchen. And it was for rent.

I had already peeked through the windows the night before after reading the ad for it in the newspaper. The rent was three hundred dollars, it had two bedrooms, and was perfect for my boyfriend and me.

I was twenty, and had moved out a couple months before to live with said boyfriend and seven of his friends, most of whom were in punk bands, one of whom would boil a massive cast-iron pot full of beans, stick it in the refrigerator that had no shelves, and eat from it for a week. When it was time for a new batch of beans, he'd pull the pot from the fridge and take it directly back to the stovetop, not bothering to make a pit stop in the sink for a meeting with soap before boiling up another week's worth.

I didn't mind living with eight boys and the collective six dogs, two pythons, a monitor lizard, and a collection of other pets we probably never realized we had. One by one, however, the boys moved out until it was just my boyfriend and me, although it took me until this moment to realize I was most likely the reason they all split. Boys don't want to share bathrooms with girls.

It was time for us to move into something for just the two of us, six of us if you counted the dogs, python, and lizard that were left when everyone else moved out. And the two-bedroom brick bungalow was it. I knew it the moment I drove up to look at it.

I made an appointment to see the house with the property manager that day after lunch with my mother. I was so excited that I could talk about nothing else during lunch: my very first house . . . with my own furniture, my own backyard, my own kitchen. I already had paint colors picked out and ideas about decorating.

"Why don't I go with you?" my mother suggested. "I don't have anything planned for the afternoon."

We headed over to the house, and in the bright light of day, I thought it was even more adorable. The wooden sash windows sparkled, the lawn gleamed emerald, and I could easily see past-due notices from credit card companies being mailed to me there. It was perfect.

The property manager was waiting for us outside with what appeared to be a friend, and I introduced my mom and myself. Together, we walked into the house and it was confirmed: The inside was exactly as I thought it would be. Wood floors, a little scuffed but who cares, and a brick fireplace with two bookcases flanking it. It was marvelous. I was ready to sign on the spot.

I turned around to whisper, "Isn't this fantastic?" to my

mother, but she was gone. Not behind me, not in front of me, she had vanished.

"Mom?" I said as I walked into the kitchen, which was original by the way, complete with a huge farmhouse sink and a refrigerator I was sure had at least a couple of shelves in it.

There she was, in the corner of the kitchen, her face flushed red.

"Did I raise you to be an animal?" she said, staring at me. "That's the way you want to live? Like an animal?"

"What?" I replied. "What happened?"

She pursed her lips tightly in anger, then pointed in a direction a little bit past me.

I turned around and darted my eyes everywhere, until my gaze hit the floor.

"That," my mother added in a hiss, "is a roach."

And, sure enough, behind the door, was an oblong dark corpse. But it wasn't just a roach. It was plus-sized. Like a Florida roach, the kind that fly and lift unattended puppies into the sky. It was so big I couldn't figure out how it got into the house without the aid of a dog door.

The roach was on its back in a death pose, its legs rising up into the air like twigs, casting a long, terrifying shadow from the light above.

"You can't live here," my mother insisted. "This is a hovel. It's disgusting!"

"This is a totally cute house!" I replied. "They probably just sprayed, that's why it's dead right out in the open."

"Where there is one roach, there are a thousand. They're all looking at us right now, do you know that?"

my mother said, her face deepening into crimson. "This kitchen is like the Coliseum of roaches. They are behind every single wall in here! And they will shit in every speck of food you buy!"

"Mom," I insisted, "this is a perfect house for us. I want this house. One dead roach doesn't mean the house is infested."

"Yes it does," she volleyed.

"Mom—"

"Yes it does," she shot.

"Mom—"

"Yes it does," she concluded. "If you rent this house, I will have a heart attack worrying about roaches crawling in everything you eat . . . crawling over you as you sleep, hiding in your shoes, laying eggs in your ears."

"I'll wear earplugs," I offered.

"Roaches carry cancer," she said simply. "And if you live in this house, you're going to get it."

I was about to say, "They do not! They carry cholera," but at that moment, the kitchen door swung open, and the property manager and her friend walked into the kitchen.

"Excuse us," she said as she took some papers out of a folder and put them on the counter.

"So just sign here," the manager said as she pointed to someplace on the paper. "And you can move in as soon as I get your deposit."

"Thank you!" the friend, who was not a friend at all but a rental competitor, said. "My boyfriend is going to love it!"

I saw my mother's face return to a pinkish hue, now

that the danger had passed. I had lost the house, just like that. The fireplace, bookcases, wood floor, and farmhouse sink would not ever be mine. I felt my face turning red.

My mother more tightly clutched her purse to her body as she passed the woman who would allow herself to live like an animal, and walked out of the kitchen.

"Look at that, Mom," I heard myself say out loud. "There's a huge dead roach behind the kitchen door. The kind that carries cancer."

And then I followed her out of the house.

THE YEAR MY MOTHER
CANCELED CHRISTMAS

*F*or the first time in our lives, Christmas Eve was not going to be at my mother's house.

"I've done it for forty years," my mom had announced suddenly. "Figure it out on your own."

It came as a significant shock to most of my family; how would our holiday stay intact if we changed venues? What about tradition? No one's ever decided to light a Christmas tree in front of the Empire State Building; it would be heresy! We had never had Christmas Eve anywhere else, and her announcement was very much akin to my mother canceling the holiday altogether.

What were we supposed to do now, gather at the buffet at Outback, my parents' favorite restaurant (but only before 5:00 P.M.), or, even worse, meet up in the parking lot of the casino where she'd suggested we have Thanksgiving? If we started having milestone events at the casino, I had no idea what the future held for my family, but if this was the direction we were heading, it wasn't good and could only involve myriad single-wides on a dirt lot some-where in West Phoenix with a cardboard sign that said "Notaro Village" in Sharpie, nailed to the mailbox. And possibly a communal outhouse.

But my baby sister, Lisa, took it in stride. She simply shrugged and said, "So? Let's just have Christmas at my house."

"Do you—do you think we're . . . allowed?" I stammered.

"Why not?" Lisa said. "She was the one who said she was sick of being everyone's Christmas servant. In my book, that leaves it wide open."

I thought about it for a minute and it seemed plausible. Why couldn't we have it at Lisa's house? Our traditional Christmas Eve antipasto was easy enough to re-create. I knew where all of the good Italian delis in town were. I knew how to make roasted peppers and garlic in olive oil; I could roll up prosciutto and soppressata. It could actually be like Christmas!

Until my sister said, "And I'm thinking about making this thing I had at a restaurant that was so good. It was Brie baked in blueberries!"

Brie and blueberries, the hair standing up on my neck screamed. Not only are we changing locales but we're also introducing unknown variables? I began to panic. Didn't she know how this might tip the balance of the holiday dynamic? Everything had been the same, exactly the same, on Christmas Eve for as long as I knew it. We used the same plates. We sat in the same seats. We had the same arguments, although the subject of Jill Biden's promiscuity was a new topic introduced in 2012, a product of residual anger left over from the election, and we had to clear the room of everyone under eighteen.

And now, Brie and blueberries? That might knock us out of orbit, only to end up at the casino next year! It wasn't Italian, I knew that, but what nationality are blueberries?

I looked at my sister, and she was so excited. She had just taken on a lot, I knew, and if need be, I thought, I could do damage control once my mother saw the new dish on the antipasto spread. I would take the blame. She hates me the most, anyway, and I could just say that I borrowed the recipe from my husband's kin, who have been in the United States for so long that they are an eighth of everything, including Pilgrims, Holler Folk, Slave Owners, Abolitionists, Sharecroppers, and People Who Eat Cornbread. It was the cornbread faction that made my mother cry when I got engaged.

As my sister and I set everything up for dinner that Christmas Eve, she pulled the Brie and blueberries out of the oven. It looked delicious. She placed it in the very center of the table, within eyeshot of everyone. I knew this had the potential of a Jill Biden–type evacuation of the young, and I just crossed my fingers that we could get past this potential disaster without wills being redrawn and paternity tests challenged (which is always Plan A with the cornbread side of the family).

I waited nervously as the rest of our family arrived and assembled around the table, ready to dig into the antipasto. It was then that I watched my mother do a double take when she saw something that wasn't a cured meat in front of her. She leaned forward, raised a brow, and sniffed.

"Get the kids," I whispered to my sister, whose eyes suddenly went wide. "This thing is gonna blow."

But my mother, instead of furrowing her brow and looking for a dishtowel to use as a whip, picked up a cracker and dipped it in the blueberries.

I held my breath as she chewed, trying to figure out if people wearing natural fibers could even pass the dress code of the casino. I was going to have to get some gold bracelets and ask relatives still in New Jersey for makeup tips, and I might have to procure a clothing item in a leopard-skin pattern.

My mother glanced up, and looked me in the eye for a moment.

Oh god, I thought, feeling chilled. Am I going to have to start smoking again? And saving my quarters?

And then she picked up a second cracker, scooped up some Bric and blueberries, and went in for another bite.

"You know what would be better?" my mother said, and I instantly drew in a breath.

I hesitated, prepared to run, then asked, "What?"

She chewed a moment as she thought. "More blueberries," she finally said.

THE SPAGHETTI LEVEL
OF RELATIONSHIP

I placed the bowl of spaghetti on the table directly in front of my husband. Then I stood there for a moment and gave him a dirty look, just like I do every time I make spaghetti.

"So," I said in a completely serious tone, "is this magic bowl of spaghetti sending you a message? Because if the pasta is trying to tell you something, I think we need to clear it up right now before I bring the meatballs out."

And then I waited.

"I'd rather not talk about it," he usually says, which is the right answer.

I'm sure not everyone eats spaghetti like this, but it's become something of a custom in our house. The gravy is homemade; the meatballs are the result of generations of meat and cheese mashing until they are perfect. I'm a pro at making gravy now, but when I was in my twenties it wasn't such an easy task. Although I'd been watching my Nana make gravy since I was old enough to know that hot oil will pop into your eye if you stand too close to frying spheres of meat, it took a certain amount of chutzpah to take on the duty myself. One afternoon, I decided to give it a shot and followed my Nana's directions for Sunday gravy, mapped out in her formal script on a stained recipe card (see page 146).

I rolled the meatballs out perfectly, a precise combination of beef, pork, breadcrumbs, garlic, and Parmesan. My Nana's recipe. Fried to a crispy, deep brown, I plopped them into the gravy, which had been waiting patiently in a pot next to the frying pan.

From the aroma steaming up from the popping bubbles in the simmering sauce, I could tell it was going to be awesome. This was my family's age-old mainstay tomato sauce for all things Italian: lasagna, eggplant parm, and, most important, macaroni. My Nana's gravy acumen left a lot to live up to. It takes hours to make, and the longer it simmers, the better it is. I left my gravy on all morning, and thought that as long as I was going through the trouble for my own dinner, I might as well spread the glory of gravy around and put together a nice lunch for a guy I had just started dating. Instead of eating off the roach coach, he would have an awesome dish of spaghetti and meatballs.

When the gravy was finished, I assembled the spaghetti and meatballs together in a Tupperware bowl and brought it to his place of employment, eager to deliver such a delicious lunch. He smiled when he took it, and said he would call me later that night. I waited in wild anticipation of what he would say. Italian girls have a lot to make up for; if you're not willing to have hot wax poured over ninety percent of your body, you'd better be exceptional in other areas. I was hoping gravy would be mine.

And he did call when he said he would, then invited me over. He made no mention of the spaghetti, but as soon as I got to his house, his reaction couldn't have been more spectacular.

He broke up with me. I tried to take it on the chin, but I sobbed to Stevie Nicks songs the whole way home, wailing like a cat. He said he wasn't ready for something so serious, not even when I insisted that macaroni was just macaroni and not an offering of a dowry. It was not a cow or a herd of goats. It was just *lunch*.

I'm sorry, he said. I'm not ready for the spaghetti level of relationship, he explained. Spaghetti added a lot of pressure. It was too soon; spaghetti was . . . more than he could do at the moment. Spaghetti was heavy.

I was stunned for days. Would it have been different with macaroni and cheese? Should I have delivered a burrito? After overthinking my misstep too much, I started to resent the spaghetti. I was never going to make it again.

I told my Nana what had happened, and she just laughed. "What a *gavone*," she said with a wave of her hand. "Spaghetti is just spaghetti! Now, if you made gnocchi or braciole, that's asking for a commitment."

I ran into him at my favorite bar that weekend and instead of snubbing him, I addressed the issue head-on.

"Hey, you," I said, wagging a drunk finger in his face. "That gravy wasn't just for you, you know. I was trying to be nice. Try to find another girl who makes it like I do.

Never. Gonna. Happen. That's my Nana's gravy, buster. And you've had it for the last time."

"It was delicious," he admitted.

Twenty years later, I still think of that guy when I make gravy. I've gotten better at it, and now, after two decades of practice, I have it nearly down to perfection. I feel almost sorry for him, but then I remember the snot bubble I blew near the freeway exit to my house twenty years ago and I just have to laugh at his foolishness. Jerk.

And when I ask my husband if he sees anything in the magic spaghetti, he never has an answer. But he eats every last bite.

THE PILE

September 30, Eugene, Oregon

Saw the first leaf fall today. It was followed by a second, then a third. By end of day, thirty to forty little veiny leaf corpses scattered all over my lawn like the bones of summer. It has begun.

I can do nothing but look away, knowing what is to come.

October 4

The lawn guys arrived, complete with leaf blowers. It is clear by their precise movements and determination to get every single leaf in a pile that they are excited to use their lawn toys for the first time this season. They spend an inordinate amount of time next to my office window, so much that I can smell the exhaust. Reminds me of the story about my dad's lawn guys, who had an eighty-year-old man operating the leaf blower, and he stepped into the pool by accident. Immediately sinking to the bottom because of the engine strapped to his back, he never made a sound, never made a splash, and resembled an old-timey diver at the bottom of a fish tank. The other leaf-blower guys just kept blowing until my dad ran out of the house and dove into the pool to rescue him. It took four men to pull him out.

That story makes me laugh until I cry.

Lawn guys make a tiny, neat pile of leaves and place it in the street in front of my house.

It is cute. I cannot help but smile.

It is The Pile.

October 5

Every leaf blown away yesterday by lawn guys has reappeared; the nice little pile is gone. Fall is back. I feel the joyful urge to place a pumpkin on my porch and a woven cornucopia with an autumnal-plaid ribbon springing from it. Make note to get a forty-percent-off coupon from Michaels and try to secure some decorative festivities, then come to the conclusion, in five seconds, that hunting through the Sunday paper, finding the coupons, then driving to Michaels, purchasing the pumpkin, and then going to the car to put on my disguise to go back in and buy the cornucopia with my second coupon would eat my autumnal seasonal spirit. The daffodils will be up in March. The neighbors will have to be happy with that.

October 11

Yard guys are back again. The Pile is bigger. Enough to bury a small body under. Pile now joined by friends of leaves. And distant cousins. Rotten teenagers walking home step off the sidewalk to kick leaf pile that can in no way defend itself. I wish curable, but annoying, sexually transmittable diseases on them all.

October 12

Rains. The Pile is flattened, leaves still falling. Leaves now joined by others they haven't seen since they budded. Those straggler leaves are inviting other leaves from trees not in my yard. Renegade leaves blowing down the street also seem to stop by to join the leaf party in front yard. Shaggy leaves missing stems or tips seem to be joining the congregation. I suspect homeless leaves; other yards must be full.

October 18

The Pile regains shape, big enough to bury a teenager under. The shortest lawn crew guy is unaccounted for. I am concerned for him, but not really enough to go poking through rotten leaves that could have slugs on them. That should be left to his boss.

October 19

STORM! A tornado of leaves whips across the yard bringing twigs, lichen, and more leaves in a tumbling display of chaos. The Pile sits still; whatever touches it sticks, unable to release itself from the hulking, gluey, decomposing hill of once vibrant foliage. It smells of earth and must. I check calendar for city leaf pickup date in my neighborhood.

November 30 to December 6.

I gasp in horror and shake my head in denial.

The Pile is up to my knees.

October 23

Someone parks on The Pile. Wheels spin for fifteen minutes to try and get vehicle to move. I spy behind curtain in front room while girl with pink hair who has an appointment at the nail salon around the corner learns a valuable life lesson. As in "Park your shitty Toyota Tercel elsewhere." I grin as her wheel wells fill with flipped-up clumps of decay and her anger is expressed as she pushes harder and harder on the gas pedal. I am giddy with joy; The Pile has her trapped. May she go back and tell her nail salon sistren to avoid The Pile; it made her late for spray tan session! Finally, after gouging troughs in The Pile with her bald tires, she shoots off the slick of leaves like she's on a pair of skis and narrowly misses hitting an oncoming Subaru Forester. She shall not return to my side of the street.

October 25

The yard guys return, and reshape and tend The Pile into the glorious mass that it is. No one on this street has a pile this size; it is alone in its striking height and width. It can now accommodate a family of four, and is now far past my knees. Of the yard guys, there is still no sign of the little one.

October 26

Mailman attempts to cross The Pile as wagon trains tried to cross the Sierra Nevada in winter. He is ill equipped, and despite his cape and costume of blue, he is bogged down in the middle, and has to stop and catch his breath before attempting the final leg of his foolishness.

You cannot beat The Pile.

House always wins.

October 27

CRISIS! CRISIS!

At 2:40 in the afternoon, I rush out of the house in an attempt to make it to FedEx to ship photographs to New York overnight. The cutoff to ship is 3:00 P.M.: I have twenty minutes to make it. I am convinced I can do it until I see The Pile, dissected and torn apart in several large chunks in front of my driveway that, unless I quickly trade my Prius in for a monster truck, I cannot get over. Time is ticking as I stare at The Pile, torn in massive clumps that have been dragged under a very low car (I suspect my neighbor's maid, who drives an El Camino) to their new resting place. I have no tools. I have no time to get tools. I use what is at my disposal, which are my feet. In my cowboy boots, I begin kicking at the satellite piles to get them out of the way, but the leaves are wet and heavy and compressed, and I sense a massive knee injury racing my way, due to arrive in approximately two minutes. But I keep kicking. And kicking. And provide a soundtrack to my efforts that is saltier than anything ever unfurled on a dock. I swear vengeance. I demean their ancestors. I curse their progeny. I wonder, so that all my neighbors can hear, how daft do you need to be to park on a pile of leaves as tall as a first-grader? As big as most European cars?

I hear shuffling behind me, and I ignore it, sure it is a cop called to come and silence the insane woman swearing and kicking at leaves in the middle of the street. "Need a hand?" is what I hear, and it is my thirty-year-old neighbor, Ed, who has a back not yet destroyed by sciatica or bulging disks. In his hand is a shovel.

I nearly collapse with relief. Together, we kick and shovel the clumps of errant leaves back to the mother pile. We are both sweaty, angry, and set on developing a lookout plan from both sides of the street to prevent this atrocity from happening again, and I have two minutes to get to FedEx.

Only because I am filled with rage and fueled by fury do I make it literally in the nick of time. And on the way home, I see a solution. I see it everywhere, because most of our little town in under construction.

I make a note of where the construction cones are located and their proximity to street corners to enable a speedy getaway in the darkness of night.

When I tell my husband of my plan, he threatens to call the police on me himself, or my doctor. My choice.

I explain that it is only a seasonal theft, and I will return the cones from whence they came when the leaf pickup has been completed, and we are out of danger.

He does not share my logic.

I make a promise not to steal traffic cones.

October 28, 2:00 A.M.

I wake abruptly with a brilliant idea and run downstairs to my computer.

YES, AMAZON SELLS TRAFFIC CONES.

But I need them now. I cannot wait two days for Prime shipping.

I have another brilliant idea.

YES, HOME DEPOT SELLS TRAFFIC CONES.

And yes, my closest Home Depot has them in stock.

I get dressed.

October 28

While I understand it is always too early to deal with the first customer of the day, I am nevertheless shocked when the man in the orange apron does not know where to find traffic cones. Together, we search every aisle until he simply vanishes on the screw aisle just as I'm getting to the part where Ed comes to rescue me with his shovel. On the next aisle, I find a nice older lady who does know where the traffic cones are and leads me right to them. However, when I turn around to demonstrate how I had to kick the leaves, there is no one there. I wonder if she was ever real.

An hour later, I have placed the bright orange cones—with my address written prominently in black Sharpie—to guard and protect The Pile until the holy day comes when they are scooped up to leaf heaven.

October 30

A cone is stolen.

I return to Home Depot.

Cashier begins talking to another cashier when I get to the part that demands an answer when I declare, "WHO would steal a cone with MY address on it?"

November 1

It is possible that there are only twenty-nine more days until leaf pickup arrives. The lawn guys are here and amass a mountain of leaves as high as an American car with an NRA sticker on the back window.

November 5

There is not a leaf left on a tree anywhere on my street, but still, they come. Every morning there are more leaves on the lawn. I'm beginning to think that others are aban-

doning their leaves here, unable to deal with the responsibility and the commitment of having trees and their
consequences.

November 7

I find a leaf in my underwear.

November 8

The lawn guys are here. They have stopped trying to
reach the top of The Pile with the leaves and just add them
to the base, which is now spreading into the traffic portion of the street.

I dare anyone to say anything to me.

November 9

I chase away a woman driving a Tahoe and her baby in
the backseat who believe they can conquer the mountain.

I run out into the yard and catch her just as she is about
to run over a cone. I walk in front of her, my hand raised
in the international sign for "STOP."

She leans out her window and asks if something is
wrong.

"There is a temporary suspension of parking here," I
say. "The cones symbolize that."

She says she doesn't see a sign.

"This is your sign," I say, and pick up a cone. "You almost just ran over it. It was nine ninety-nine."

"That's not a sign," she replies. "That's a cone."

"There are no signs on police barricades," I retort. "Are you going to run through those?"

She rolls her eyes at me and backs up, makes a U-turn, and parks on the other side of the street before she and her baby march off to get her nails done. When she is safely around the corner, I pelt the side of her car with a handful of leaves.

Whore.

November 11

Some agent of the devil has not only driven through the corner of The Pile, but has taken one cone with it and shot the other cone into my neighbor's yard. The carnage is spread across the street in a grisly arc. If I were an expert at tire tracks, I would say that they were those of a Tahoe. They certainly match the ones I found on Google.

In defiance, I leave them there as a reminder of foolery.

I return to Home Depot, and buy a replacement cone *plus a backup.*

November 15

The lawn guys are here. They have brought all of the leaves from the one-hundred-foot-tall Oregon ash tree in the backyard into the front. The Pile now stretches in front of my entire front yard, creating a ridge and a screen of privacy that I particularly like. When the yard crew departs, I cross in front of the living room windows in my tights. I find three leaves inside the front door. I put my skirt back on.

Sometimes, when I wake up in the middle of the night, I hear the blower. It is far away, but I can hear it.

November 20

My sister mocks me when she asks me, in a phone conversation, what is new and I mention that in ten more days, The Pile might be gone.

"You are posting far too much about The Pile on Facebook," she warns me. "And on Twitter. You have thirty-four pictures on Instagram of its various stages of gestation. Nobody cares about The Pile. Even I stopped 'liking' the posts about The Pile. The picture of the squirrel on it was cute until you mentioned that you threw rocks at it."

"You don't even know what you're talking about," I reply. "We grew up in Arizona. The only things that collected en masse were tumbleweeds. You've never seen a real tree in your entire life, let alone had to deal with them."

"I've seen a tree," she shot back. "I've seen a tree!"

"Can you tell me the difference between a maple and an oak?" I asked her. "Which ones have acorns? Which ones have little wingy-spinny things fly off of them? Which ones peel? Because there's a tree that peels, you know. Just like if you spend fifteen minutes outside in Phoenix without sleeves and sunblock on."

"If I could 'unlike' this conversation right now, I

would," she said. "Please stop talking about The Pile. Big deal about a couple of leaves."

"A couple of leaves?" I screamed. "A couple? I have a hundred-year-old sycamore tree in my front yard. I also have a willow that is sixty feet tall. Not to mention the monster Oregon ash in the backyard that you like to put your hammock under when it's still beautiful and in bloom. You're not here when the tree starts to get naked. You don't know what the story's like *now,* sister. I'm living in a *season,* I'll have you know. I have about four hundred pounds of wet, rotting leaves in front of my house, and if someone parks on those leaves or blocks access to The Pile when the city comes to take them away, I am stuck with them. STUCK. There are no second chances here. I got one shot at this, baby. And I am *taking* it."

"Did you just call me *baby*?" she asked.

"I gotta go," I said quickly. "Someone is acting suspicious around my cones."

November 24

I saw the earthmover six streets away.

Six streets away.

November 26

Today might have been Thanksgiving.

November 28

When I washed my hair today, three leaves fell out that I didn't know were there. One of them had a slug on it.

November 30

Nothing.

December 1

I heard the earthmover stop in front of my house, but it was just a semi delivering a new dishwasher to my neighbor. I kept my cool. I kept it. I only yelled at the delivery guys to hurry up twice.

December 2

Utter silence.

December 3

Out of milk since the first, and the only things we have left to eat in the house are freezer-burned egg rolls and Cream of Wheat.

I'm fine with that.

December 4

The unthinkable has happened. I'm out of Belgian chocolate toffee creamer for my coffee. I can live without cookies and soda and dinner, but I cannot live without coffee, and I can't drink my coffee without Belgian chocolate toffee creamer. I can literally see Safeway from my deck, and if I were truly a thinking person, I would have had a zip line installed years ago. I calculate, second by second, how long it will take me to drive the twenty feet to Safeway, get my creamer, and get back: nine minutes, thirteen seconds, and that's if I can find a parking space in the first or second row, and if the mummy in front of me isn't writing a check or paying for her Ensure with dimes.

What are the chances that the leaf pickup will arrive after I leave and be gone before I come back? Slim, I decide. Slim. But not slim enough that I shouldn't do some recon first, and that involves driving the car around a three-block area to see if the earthmover is in the vicinity. If it is, I will go back home. If it's not, I'm off to get creamer. I decide to take the chance. I decide I will risk it.

So I get my stuff and I lock the front door, and as soon as I turn around, there she is. There she is. Pink hair. Toyota Tercel.

I don't even finish turning the key in the lock before I am marching over toward her and her car, pointing at her and yelling, "No. No. No," because she has returned to get her nails done again and parked not on The Pile, because it's way too big, but just close enough to it that the earthmover will not have any room to come in and scoop the leaves up.

"Absolutely not," I say as she gets out of her car with a smirk on her face. "Absolutely not."

She doesn't say anything, doesn't even look at me, but gets out of her car and closes the door.

"You are going to move that car," I say. "What do you think this is? What do you think these cones are for? Is this a carnival? Do I look like I'm selling tickets to you?"

She looks at me, cocks her little pink head to one side, and says, "You can't tell me where to park. I can park anywhere I want. I have two hours before I even get a ticket."

I nod at her. Then I nod some more. I bite the inside of my lip and my ears go cold. My fingers turn to ice, my neck is freezing. I feel myself start to tremble.

"No," I say. "No, I can't tell you where to park. But I can suggest to you that if you do not move your car elsewhere, if you insist on leaving your car right in that very spot, not only will you come back here with a whole different strain of nail fungus than you already have, but your car"—and I point to it—"will be under *that*." And then I point to The Pile.

"And if you don't think I am batshit crazy enough to do it," I said, and pulled out my cellphone, "then you can ask my doctor."

She stood there for a moment, then whipped around and opened her car door, but before she got in shouted, *"You are nuts!"*

"Get out of here before I make you wear this!!" I said as I picked up a cone and waved it at her like a torch.

I had just put the cone back down when I heard the rumble, felt the ground shake.

Then I heard it.

Beep. Beep. Beep.

It was like hearing angels sing.

I turned around and there it was, coming straight toward me, right for The Pile. The earthmover.

It was leaf pickup day at last.

I picked up my cones and hugged them to my chest. I waved to the driver, who did not return my wave. But I didn't care.

We had done it.

The dump truck was right behind him, and as the first scooper went in and lifted a section of The Pile that was so dense and compact that not one single leaf fluttered off, I knew I had done it.

It took them three minutes to remove The Pile, and when they had cleared my driveway, I went to the store and got Belgian chocolate toffee creamer, milk, and whatever else I wanted.

When I got home, I was still smiling, especially when I saw the spot in front of my house where The Pile had been. I could no longer wear tights in the living room, but I hardly cared.

I had just gotten to my front door when Sara, my new neighbor, walked over with her hands in the air.

"I missed it?" she cried. "I missed it! What do I do with all of these leaves now?" she asked.

I shook my head and sighed. "You're going to have to wait for the next pickup in a month," I informed her sadly.

"Some jerk parked on my pile," she said, and as I looked over to Sara's curb, there was the Toyota Tercel, sitting on Sara's leaves as if it were about to lay a big turd egg.

"I'm going to leave them a nasty note," Sara proclaimed.

"Oh, no," I said, putting my groceries down as I put my arm around her and we walked toward the street. "We're going to do much better than that. You have much to learn, my new friend. Let's talk about cones. . . ."

TIMBER

I had always wanted to live in an ivy-covered cottage.

It was at the very top of my dream list, along with winning an Oscar, or dieting my Fred Flintstone feet back down to a size seven.

But some wishes will never come true, and long ago I learned to be happy with the fact that they even make shoes in my size, and that for now, I can still afford cable to watch the Oscars.

Other wishes can't wait to come true, and require so little to become reality, such as eighteen continuous rainy days and forty-mile-per-hour winds.

It is always beneficial if you are not naked when your dream comes true, unless it involves a Tom of the Hiddleston or Hardy variety. Sometimes, however, before you know it, you have just stepped foot into the shower when the wish fairy swirls her magic wand and from the far end of the house, you feel a giant THUD shake your universe, and for a moment, you believe in Godzilla, and that he has, indeed, just made it across the Pacific.

"HONEY!" I heard my husband scream. "Did you fall out of the shower again?"

Because naturally, when I feel my house shake, I suspect Godzilla is slamming against it, but my husband suspects me.

"No!" I yelled back. "But I'll be right down!"

I threw on my pajamas, which stuck all over me because I didn't have time to dry off, and ran downstairs. My husband was busy going from room to room, but I shot out the back door immediately. At first, I didn't see it, but I did wonder why a streamer of ivy was stretched across the back deck.

And then, as my mind slowly put the puzzle together, I saw it.

I knew that goddamned tree was going to fall on my house.

I had been saying it for years. Although the forty-foot oak had provided glorious shade on the south side of my yard, where I put a chaise lounge and read my summer afternoons away, there was no doubt that someday it was going to come crashing through my roof into my bedroom, crushing me in between beams and my foam mattress like a Hostess cherry pie.

The tree had been deceased since we had moved in ten years ago, but it stood in a line of magnificent oaks and poplars that lined the side of my neighbor's yard. Sitting on her deck, it felt like you were in a tree house, surrounded by leaves and ivy. Lots of ivy.

The ivy, it turned out, was the only thing holding the tree up. For fifty years, the vine had twisted and crept up the trunk, growing stronger, and thicker, and splitting off into new rivers of ivy that twirled and curled over the trunk and branches of the oak. By the time we had moved in, the ivy had completely covered most of the tree, and gave the illusion that it was alive and doing well. It even fooled the pair of raccoons that built a nest there. In fact, I didn't even know the tree was an oak because it had no leaves and had always simply been a massive tree trunk that towered over everything.

But now the tree, its ivy, and the raccoon apartment had fallen on the entire south side of my house, spanning the forty feet from its trunk to the new hole in my roof.

When I got to the front yard, my neighbor Louise was standing across the street with her hand over her mouth. All she could do was point to the side of my house. I waved to her as I walked over to my neighbors, who were now missing a giant tree and needed to call their insurance company to come and lift it off my house.

I felt quite awkward doing this; it was seven o'clock in the morning, and all of their lights were out. Clearly, the tree had taken down their power line with it in the fall, and I was sure they'd want to get the power company out right away to fix it.

Which was not going to be fun for them. Several years ago, one of the tree limbs in our backyard came crashing down during a storm, leaving a live wire on the ground and our house cold and dark. It was twelve degrees outside, and the snow was still falling. We were so grateful when the power company's truck pulled up and the line guy jumped out. We waited, staring up at the ceiling, for our lights to turn back on, mainly because I had a book due in a week. Then we heard a truck door shut, and the power truck zoomed off.

"Wait! Stop! I only have one chapter to go!" I shouted from behind the window as the truck stopped at the end of our block, then made a right turn, and vanished.

I called the power company immediately on my rotary phone (I have four), and was informed that the truck had only stopped by to cut my power off. For *their* safety. As for when they might return to turn the power back on, we were told we were now at the bottom of a very long list of people who already knew that the power company is only in a rush to come to your house when they don't need to do anything but disconnect you.

For the next six days, and with the aid of two very long extension cords from our neighbors on either side, we huddled in our living room with two space heaters, a lamp, and my iPad. I finished the book before our power was turned back on, but had to walk to Starbucks to email it because our car was still frozen in ice. Bundled in layer upon layer that was topped with a thick wool shawl and my hair in a bun (there was no way I was going to sacrifice a space heater in place of a hair dryer), I was spotted on the back deck by one of my neighbors as I was taking out the trash.

"How are you guys doing?" he called. "Are you rehearsing for a play?"

It was the longest six days of my life. I couldn't imagine surviving it with three kids. I did not envy my poor neighbors one bit.

I knocked on the door to inform them about their tree and their new status as "powerless," and it took several minutes for my neighbor, Sara, to answer. I had clearly woken her up. Now, I was in my jammies and she was in her jammies, but one of us looked like she was modeling activewear for J. Crew, and one of us looked like Baby Jane Hudson in flannel. I'm sure I even looked drunk, since every night while I'm sleeping, one of my eyebrows walks off my face and never comes back and my hair takes on the semblance of writhing snakes.

But on the other side of that door was blond, slim, perky Sara with her hair in a messy ponytail that I saw on Pinterest, which took me forty minutes to attempt and fail, making me look more like the elderly lady in my neighborhood who walks around wearing a wedding dress and dragging a suitcase than a cute little mom of three who opens up her front door at seven in the morning looking impeccably and adorably disheveled. She didn't even have bad breath. She made yoga pants look . . . good.

"I'm sorry to wake you up so early," I apologized right away. "But one of the trees in your backyard is now in my backyard, and it's kinda on my roof. And I think your electricity is out."

"Oh, I thought I heard something," she replied, and reached over to turn on the porch light, which immediately shone brightly. "Nope. Our electric is on. I'll call the insurance company when they open. I'm so sorry."

"I'm sorry I woke you, but I was afraid there might be a live wire in your backyard," I explained. "Can I . . . just see . . . the back of your hair?"

"Okay . . ." Sara said, slowly turning her head.

Just as I thought.

"It's . . . super cute," I said, nodding, and because I felt that my PJ bottoms had inched up my ass crack since I was still rather damp when I put them back on, I backed down the front porch facing her.

"I'll call you when I know something," she said.

I waved and smiled, determined not to give her a rear view if I could help it.

I got back to my house just in time to see the power company's truck shoot away from my house and down the street.

"Oh no," I cried. "Oh no, oh no, oh no!"

"We're dark," my husband confirmed when I came back into the house. "They cut us 'just in case' our wire was live. You'd better get your Ingalls gear on again. It's going to be a long week."

As soon as the clock hit nine, I was on the phone to State Farm to see what they could do to help us.

"I know that it's my neighbor's tree, so it will be their claim—" I started, but the agent interrupted me.

"It's an act of God," she said.

This was no time to try missionary or conversion tactics on me. I didn't need to be reminded that there was a forty-foot tree on my house because I was a shitty person. I already knew that. Besides, I had just earned some karma when I told Sara the back of her head looked cute. Maybe God could take it down a notch and just knock a thirty-foot tree on my house the next time.

"I was raised Catholic, but I'm lapsed, and I gotta say

it's just not my thing, okay?" I stated. "I watch *NOVA. I am a science person.*"

But then she went on to tell me something that defies even science: Even though my neighbor's dead tree, which had been dead for as long as the day I set eyes on it, fell on my house, it was not my neighbor's fault.

Somehow, it was mine. And if your neighbor's dead tree falls on your house, it will be yours. "Act of God" is apparently all the insurance company needs to say to make you liable, but I don't even understand what that means. Which god? Which god threw a four-story-tall log wrapped in ivy on my house? Was it Zeus? Apollo? Elvis? Which one was having a bad Almighty day?

Can you give me a hint, I wanted to ask her, because I want to draw a politically incorrect cartoon about them and send it to *The New Yorker.*

I did not know that insurance companies had to adhere to whether something was God-related before they paid for the damage that your policy says they will. Now, a plague of locusts, okay, that was mentioned in the Bible; I can see the clause there. A bush catching fire in your front yard, again, it was forewarned; a flood that destroys the sin of man, all right, I'll give it to you. But where in the Bible do trees fall on houses? If a fireball caused it, we have the precedent of Sodom and Gomorrah, but there was no meteor, fireball, or space junk involved here.

Frankly, I didn't care anyway, because God did not knock my tree down. I am certain Mary would have intervened, saying, "Goddamnit, you have already thrown thirty trees down there and crushed a woman to death like a cherry pie. Take some Miralax and put that shit to bed. So what if Laurie promised if you let her win the sixth-grade relay race on field day that she would become a nun, and she forgot all about that when she started dating? It was field day. If it was the Olympics or a football game, I'd say, 'Throw that friggin' tree, a promise is a promise,' but seriously. She got a bad rash down there because of that race, remember. She even has a rash right now."

If you asked Stephen Hawking what knocked my tree down, I'm pretty sure he'd say it was physics. The wind, plus heavy rain, plus rotted tree roots is why I had a tree on my house, which also is why I now did not have electricity. And *that* was an act of the power company.

"And your deductible is one thousand eight hundred sixty-five dollars," the insurance agent added, which was enough to finish all of the dental work I needed but would now go toward getting a dead tree that did not belong to me off of my house.

State Farm did send a team of guys out to cut the tree into chunks to see what kind of damage had occurred underneath on the roof.

It turns out that the tree not only collapsed in my yard but impaled my roof, tore down the fence, crushed the gate, and left decades of twisted ivy in piles three feet deep and thirty feet long on the side of my house, ivy so old that its circumference measured ten inches, like a python. I'm fairly sure that if we ever get the ivy removed, we will find an Aztec temple underneath it all.

By the end of the day, we had our electricity back on,

which was good, because I had another book to finish in a week. This one.

Several Sundays later, a hillbilly family responded to Sara's post on Craigslist for free firewood, and arrived with a Home Depot's worth of chain saws, chains, a winch, and three trailers.

But a month later, I still have a hole in my roof, the gate and fence are still busted, and the ivy covering one entire side of my house appears to be getting deeper. I have a feeling it's still growing, and that one or more of the hill-billies got left behind in there, trying to find their way out, because every now and then the ivy . . . rustles.

At least I can scratch the ivy-covered cottage off my dream list and replace it with another, more specific wish that doesn't have anything to do with an insurance deductible. I was all set to add my wish that science would catch up to my metabolism, and then I remembered about chemotherapy.

Right now I'm just alarmed that as my husband passed my office, he mentioned, "This deductible is high. Maybe we should cut back on a few things until we pay it off. Things like cable. You don't care about missing the Oscars, do you?"

WHERE IS HOME?

I have to admit that I had never seen anyone shoot up in front of me before. I've seen people take enormous bong hits. I saw my friend Dave search in his vomit for the pills he had just taken at a Zia Records work party. I've known people who didn't have any butter knives that weren't blackened due to their love of hash. But when it came to intravenous, straight-up mainlining it, I was a baby.

There, in a small but brightly lit alley, was a young couple getting ready to Keith Richards their way to somewhere my bottle of Tylenol PM has no access card to. As I passed by them, they didn't blink, didn't look up, and didn't care what anyone saw, as if their little space in a downtown alley was hidden from view in a giant opiate bubble.

You never know what you're going to see downtown, I reminded myself, not even when you're three hundred feet from the farmer's market.

I've spent a lot of time in downtown Phoenix: I bought a dilapidated bungalow in which homeless people were squatting in Coronado, one of the worst neighborhoods in town, that made my mother cry the first time she saw it (my mother cried every time I took her to see a house I might live in) and vow she'd burn it down before she saw one of her children live in it, and then I got a job at *The Arizona Republic.* I loved working downtown. I was a columnist with my own office, but I completely failed to negotiate a snack assistant into my contract, which meant that when it was feeding time, I burst out onto the sidewalks with thousands of other people flocking to Chipotle, even in July, when the streets of downtown become nothing less than channels of hot, steaming lava. To be honest, I loved it.

I felt like I was finally a part of a bustling city, even the parts that weren't so nice: the bodies sleeping or passed out on the sidewalks, the stink of urine in the alleys, the dirt lots that gathered trash and never had any hope to become something other than dirt lots. It was still the city, and someplace I had waited a long time to get to, even if it meant risking a third-degree burn between ample inner thighs to secure a shitty burrito from Chipotle.

Then my bosses became assholes. I was fired, and my days of downtown walking were over. That was fine. In time, my thighs began to heal, and the hair grew back. But as I looked around, I realized that Phoenix was done with me and I was done with it. I was sick of the heat, sick of the dirt lots, and sick of the assholes who were clogging up the freeway with New Jersey license plates. I wanted to live someplace green, clean, and where nobody had ever fired me before. I stuck a For Sale sign in the front yard of my downtown bungalow and moved to Oregon.

I did not take my mother with me when we looked for a house.

Everyone knows Eugene now because of the Oregon Ducks, but before that it was the home of Ken Kesey, the guy who wrote *One Flew Over the Cuckoo's Nest* and introduced the Hells Angels to LSD, and if you ever put your lips on a bong after he did, you are royalty in that town. Kesey and his friends, known as Merry Pranksters, drove a painted Partridge Family–like bus across the country in the sixties with the Grateful Dead on board and a hallucinating Neal Cassady at the wheel. A friend of mine proudly told me that her mom was dating a Merry Prankster, although now he has a farm of mini-donkeys. It's also the only place where you can win a city council election by claiming you dropped more acid with the Grateful Dead than your opponent.

Now Ken Kesey is dead, and has a square named after him in the middle of downtown, with a terrifying bronze sculpture in which he is wearing a jaunty cap and reading to several equally frozen children, most likely horrified by his tales of tripping his balls off with Hells Angels. Food trucks sell tofu wraps and meatless cheesesteak subs behind him, and every year, it's the place where zombies gather to do their *Thriller* flash-mob dance.

The downtown of Eugene has flower baskets hanging from the original streetlamps from the turn of the twentieth century, and we have medians in the middle of the two-lane streets that are filled with trees and shrubs, creating a canopy in the springtime that stretches from sidewalk to sidewalk. There are people whose only job is to water the flowers downtown. VooDoo Doughnuts sells goodies in the shapes of genitals and decorated with Cap'n Crunch. There are two stores a block apart that make furniture and accessories out of the giant trees around Eugene that have been taken down because they are too old or have been deemed too hazardous. We legalized pot and, as of now, you can buy it openly in pot stores that are called Cannabliss and Sweet Leaf, and the *Willamette Week* just advertised a position for a staff pot reviewer. I'm not kidding. My neighbor Ed is applying for it.

In Eugene, the *high* is the limit.

Eugene is green. People do not litter. It's quiet, and the worst thing that has happened to me in the last ten years is that a homeless person lived in my bushes for a winter and then took a shit in my garlic bed. There are no highway shooters because there is no highway. Once I thought a tweaker died on my lawn, but when he finally woke up and wiped the crawling ants from his eyes, he said that my yard was beautiful and that it just looked like a nice place to sleep.

Eugene was everything I was looking for when I fled Phoenix. It's rarely hot, so my inner thighs never sweat so much that I mistakenly think I peed my pants, and no one here has ever fired me, and no one hates me. I know every single person on my street. We share holidays together, and soon we are having a party for my new next-door neighbors and their three extremely well-mannered kids, to welcome them (yes, I admit this is before their tree fell on my house). He was an epidemiologist with the CDC who didn't think he was helping the world enough, so now he's a doctor at the homeless clinic. We're also bringing what we've canned this summer—I make pickles and jams; Louise, the dean of the honors college, makes chutneys from the fruit of our neighbors' trees; and Gemesa makes chocolate chip cookies with salted brown butter—to share and trade with everyone.

I have second-row seats to see Yo-Yo Ma because I nicely asked the lady at the symphony box office the day before tickets went on sale to the general public and complimented her on her hair.

Merlin, the guy who just put memory in my computer at Mac Tonic (Eugene does not have a full-service car wash, let alone an Apple Store), did not charge me for removing seventy-eight viruses and updating my iMac to 10.8.

I love Eugene.

Last week, I walked the couple blocks downtown to the farmer's market that takes up four whole streets. I brought a basket. It's all organic produce that has been picked that morning. I once saw the two mushroom dealers get into an argument about which one found the rarest mushroom ever that resulted in one of them storming off, shouting, "I don't care if you have pictures! You did NOT find a Tree Hugger next to a Gray Shaggy Parasol! It is fungally impossible!" while his rival threw a chanterelle at him to symbolize his disgust. I get a whiff of VooDoo Doughnuts making their signature delicacy, the Cock-n-Balls, and I smile. There's a young traveler sleeping on Ken Kesey's bronze lap—at least I hope he's just sleeping—and his pit bull puppy is playing with another pit bull puppy of another teenage vagabond, who is holding a sign that says "I love VooDoo Doughnuts. Buy me one."

Homeless people in Eugene seem to just want doughnuts.

Then I dip down into an alley shortcut, where a guy in his late teens has made a home out of two sewer pipes and a tarp. He is strumming on his guitar like he just snorted an entire eight ball and sings loudly, "Jack and Jill went up the hill to see if they could score. Jack came down but Jill is just a whore."

A young couple is next to him, seated against a wall, paying no attention to the pornographic nursery rhyme because they are busy. He's holding a tiny glass bottle, and she is pulling the syringe out of it and moving it to her arm.

And then, ten feet away, literally about three steps, there's a wooden cart full of bright green, red, and yellow peppers.

My first stop at the farmer's market is at the meat wagon, where they also sell fresh eggs. I notice that there's one dozen left in the case, and I say out loud, "Oh yay! He has a dozen left!" and I hear the hipster in the shiny gray shirt and man bun ahead of me in line say, "Oh yeah. And a dozen eggs."

And that's when the Phoenix girl comes out in me—the same girl who had someone try to burn down her house in Coronado three times (I have a feeling that at least two of those times it was my mom), who had a gang shooting on her street, and who once found a used condom on top of her block wall—and says, "Seriously? You're taking the last dozen because you just heard me say that?"

Then the meat guy says from behind the counter, "The eggs are five-fifty a dozen, but for six bucks, they'll go home with the winner."

And the Phoenix girl says, "They won't go home with the winner. They'll go home with the biggest asshole. And that won't be me."

Then the hipster turns to me and says, "This is not the only game in town for eggs."

It turns out it is. All the eggs are gone, so I buy some purple carrots and a jar of honey, and then I make my way to the booth of the tamale lady, the stop I have saved until last. She's from Bisbee, and she makes awesome tamales and enchilada sauce. People in Eugene put broccoli and tempeh in their burritos, and several times I almost made a citizen's arrest due to the obscenity of it all. But the ta-male lady understands, and every week, I beg her to open a restaurant that doesn't have American cheese on enchiladas.

"People here have no idea," I say, and she laughs.

"Do you miss it?" I ask her.

"Miss what?" she replies.

"The desert. The Southwest. Arizona," I answer.

"Oh sure," she says. "But I love it here."

"I love it, too," I agree. "But I just saw two kids shooting up in an alley and some asshole just stole my dozen eggs from the meat guy."

"What a jerk," she replies. "In Arizona, someone with a concealed-weapons permit would have taken those eggs back."

"My brother-in-law would have shot him," I add, and we laugh.

"But which place is home?" I ask her. "Eugene, or Arizona?"

She thinks for a minute. "Here," she finally says. "I've been here twenty-three years. It's home now."

I smile and nod. But when I think about it, when I really think about it, I can't agree. Eugene is home, as in the sense of it is where I live, where my house is, but where my home is, well, that's a different story.

My home, I know, is a three-day drive south, where people have fired me, where people hate me, where broccoli has never touched a tortilla, and where even at the end of September it is 107 fucking degrees, and I am unsure if I peed my pants or if my cooter has simply sweat that much. I'm actually hoping it's pee.

On my way out of the market, I decide to avoid the alley and take the street instead. At the stoplight is a man bun in a shiny gray shirt holding my stolen eggs, and as the light turns, he steps into the crosswalk.

"Hey," I yell after him, "I bet you're going to get salmonella from eating ill-gotten asshole eggs!" And my only wish is that I had a mushroom to throw after him.

DEAR LAURIE,
AGE TWENTY-FIVE

This is you, me, us, at age fifty. *I know!* I can't believe I've lived this long either! I'm sure you remember, since it happened like literally yesterday for you, that after a couple of drunken tumbles on the train tracks, people placed bets on your lifespan. Looks like a couple of people owe us money, but it turns out that we have actually outlived them! How awesome is that?

First, I want to thank you for not leaving me with a badly rendered tattoo, or a piercing on the face or elsewhere. I would rather have a large, obscenely colored birthmark than a Pearl Jam stick figure on my arm or an overarching bridge of roses and thorns across my chest. Thank you so much for spending most of your money on booze and cigarettes so luxuries such as lifelong mistakes made by a drunk twenty-five-year-old were never made. I love you for it. Yes, stealing five syrups from IHOP or mail from a church was ill-advised, but in comparison, you did far less damage than was ultimately possible.

So here's the deal: At the rate that technology is advancing, it's just a matter of time before you show up on my doorstep like something I might have left at a fire station in an era of frivolity. Actually, regarding that: Surprise! *You're barren!!!!!* Whore around all you want. Your ovaries are no more functional than doorknobs when it comes to reproducing, so take all of that money you're going to spend on pregnancy tests and just buy a car. You've got a way better chance of making raisins in your office than you do of anything ever attaching itself to the inside of that uterus unless that zygote is a rock climber and has a stubborn streak.

Anyway, I thought I'd beat you to the punch of time traveling because, frankly, I live in kind of a decent neighborhood now, and knowing you, you're not coming alone. There's liable to be a band in your car, with one of the guitarists bound to puke in the front yard and at least three other people in the backseat with outstanding warrants. Sure, hopefully enough time has passed when you cross through the space and time continuum for statutes of limitations to take effect, but I'll tell you right now that I'm not bailing out the guy who went to San Quentin. I'll never get my bond back, and yes, I care about things like that now. So stay put, okay? My homeowner's umbrella policy will not cover you. I've already asked. Plus the former diplomat across the street still has CIA connections. Throw a grapefruit at his Christmas decorations and all of you will be renditioned to Turkey. Or someplace worse. Like Florida.

This is what I want to tell you. I really want you to listen, because it is important. This is the most important thing I can teach you.

Don't shit where you eat. Keep your areas of preference unmarred. Do not mess them up with sex, crushes, flirting, or bounced checks. If something is important to you, don't ruin it by ruining it. Example: If you like a band, don't ruin it by sleeping with a guy in the band. If you like a restaurant, don't ruin it by sleeping with a waiter at the restaurant. If you really like hanging out at a bar, don't ruin it by sleeping with the bartender, manager, or bouncer. If you like where you work, don't ruin it by sleeping with a co-worker or your boss. If you really enjoy having someone as a friend, don't ruin it by loaning them money.

Stop dating assholes. If he can't call you back, or is already drunk on your date when you pick him up because he doesn't have a car, or sprays you on the leg with compressed air and gives you a burn because he thinks it's funny, or (and this is a good one) tells you he met a girl on the train from Portland to Seattle and he's going to hang out with her for a while, he is an asshole. If he is still living with his ex-girlfriend, he is an asshole. If he is caught kissing another girl in a closet at a Christmas party, he is an asshole. If you see him banging his own head against a fence because he is a loser, he is a psychotic asshole. And P.S. Don't talk to the guy at the work party with the long blond hair. Just don't. It's tempting, he looks like Gregg Allman, but he is not Gregg Allman. He is worse. He is not going to break your heart for forever, I promise that, but when he flees the state it will make you miss your macroeconomics final and that is going to suck way harder. Besides, that guy now drives a school bus in Seattle, lives in an apartment, and clearly never went back to community college. Sometimes the Internet is a wonderful thing.

Always wear a slip. This is wisdom from an Old Lady Who Once Used to Go to Punk Shows, and you know that's true because that was merely years ago for you. Slips are your friends. Slips are miracles. Slips will prevent your cotton skirt from being eaten by your butt crack when you are wearing tights, as exampled by the girl in front of me in the crosswalk yesterday. Slips keep everything where it is supposed to be. Blanche DuBois wore them, Maggie the Cat wore them, and Marilyn Monroe wore them. Spanx is not enough. In addition to the squeeze, you need a protective layer of slink. I promise you, I say this with love. P.S. Spanx is something you should have invented instead of a skinny girl named Sara who is now worth sixty billion dollars. You wore it first, sugar. You wore it first.

You're not as smart as you think you are. I'm sorry, but it's true. You don't even pay for your own car insurance yet. Sure, you've taken a psych class at community college and some art history courses, but your life experience is just starting. No one really cares what Monet painted and why, and you're never going to understand the makings of a narcissist until you meet one. And you will. Don't get in a fight with Pop Pop about Hiroshima no matter what you think is moral or not. You only saw pictures of the war; he spent three years in Europe fighting it. And stop, this very moment, saying the "R" word. One of your best friends is going to have a sweet little baby with Down syndrome who is going to light up your fucking world and make you want to punch yourself for every time you said it. And it's a lot.

Here's the thing: Every single day, you will learn something. It might be not to pay one credit card with another, or it might be that on Charnelton and West Twentieth Avenue, there's a rise in the sidewalk that will bring you down every single time. It might be that meat goes bad after five days in the fridge and not to serve it to guests. It might be that you really don't need to wait for the hippie blocking the freezer section you need to access while he reads the ingredients on every single box on the third shelf; you might just say, "Excuse me," and move on in. It might be that arriving on time feels way better than making your friends wait ten minutes to order appetizers. Either way, your knowledge grows every day that you are alive, and by now, I know 9,125 more things than you do, literally twice as much. Which means that the people you may not think have a pulse on what's going on know all too well what's important and what's not. Old people are not creepy. They are living libraries of experience. *Use them.*

All right. This next part is going to be hard. Please take a deep breath.

Everything goes gray.

Everything.

But getting older isn't all bad; there are a lot of good parts, too. Because you still wear tights every day, most of the hair on your legs is rubbed off like on the calves of old men who wear socks for eighty years.

That's awesome, right?

You can afford to buy nicer shoes, and when the soles of your boots wear out, you won't have to wrap them with electrical tape anymore. You can pay a cobbler to fix them for twenty bucks.

You like Indian food. You really do. When you had curry that time in 1985, it was made by a hippie who had absolutely no idea what she was doing. Seriously. Six tablespoons of cumin, a carrot, and some yogurt is not, and will never be, curry. Try it again. Preferably made by someone who knows where India is.

Don't waste time on books that suck. You have my absolute permission to abandon a book or movie that is not lighting you on fire. I don't care who wrote it or that she was shortlisted for a Pulitzer for it. It is not the book for you. It takes forever for the little girl to be eaten by the lion, I'm just warning you. In fact, you're going to be assigned *Orlando* next year for your Women Authors class, and it will become your Most Hated Book Ever. Do read that one. It will give you something to argue about twenty years from now at the English Department faculty parties. Other than that, employ this rule: A book gets fifty pages. If you aren't dying to get back to it the next day, move on over to the next one. There is absolutely no sense in reading an awful book when a good one is waiting for you to open it. That includes anything written by me.

You're not fat. It's true, you're not as skinny as Alicia, and, yes, Alicia will win the affections of the boy you like,

but that's not why he dumped you. He dumped you because he is stupid, and you deserve someone smarter than
a guy who will drop you when he sees someone prettier.
And skinnier. And with looser guidelines. (She'll get
drunk one night and tell you everything. You will be horrified and never look at a picnic table in a public park
again in the same way.) But it does not mean you are fat.
You are actually pretty awesome. Don't duck out of pictures, jump into them. You are twenty-five. Thigh gap is
genetic, it is not attained, and that is not your fault. And
you won't believe this, but twenty-five years from now,
people will be getting ass implants in hopes of having a
bubble butt *exactly* like the one you have now. So cele-
brate, even if it is a little early. Your ass rocks.

Always buy a round-trip ticket. You will one day be
stuck in Seattle with an ex-boyfriend who lives with a
stripper, her baby, and her two hippie nannies with fairy
names. You will realize you've made a huge mistake in
your plans to stay and see how Seattle works out when the
stripper and her nannies spend all day making a pot of
soup (with another six tablespoons of cumin) for homeless people, then drive their van downtown to dish out the
soup without realizing that most homeless people do not
have dinnerware on their persons. Like soup bowls. Or
spoons. Seattle will not work out for you. You can still go,
but just make sure that you have a way to get back home
after your mother told you she was not going to be buying
you a plane ticket back home because actions have consequences and it is about time you learned your lesson. She
is right, but she will change her mind once you call her

with your prepaid phone card and tell her that no one in that house takes baths.

You only have room for one crazy friend at a time. Insanity requires a good deal of effort and likes to talk on the phone a lot. Therefore, you can have a crazy friend, just keep it at a maximum of one. Trips down the rabbit hole, or even a run over to T.J.Maxx with a crazy friend, can last a lifetime, especially if your friend's not done looking at every single item in the store and hides from you when it's time to go. Also, always get takeout when eating with your crazy friend, especially if drinks are involved. There will be a fight with the waitress. There is always a fight with the waitress, and food is sent back, spit in, and returned to your table. Plus sometimes they shoplift, and the last way you want to spend an afternoon is in the back office of World Market because your friend pocketed some fake turquoise earrings and a jar of Nutella. Remember, also, that there are times when you are the crazy friend to other people who have their shit more together than you do, so if your burrito is lacking cheese, suck it up.

Dad's right, you do suck at art, so major in something else. I know. Hard pill to swallow, but I'm afraid it's true. It's also true of most art majors who had parents who were too afraid to tell their children that their talents lay elsewhere. Like in retail sales. Kudos to Dad for making you major in journalism when journalism was still a career before it became advertising and public relations. Yeah. That's the shitty part. But I already told you that everything goes gray, so I'm not going to venture into the level of intelligence in the world today. There are things called blogs. I shall say no more.

You're going to get fired. More than once. More than three times. More than seven times. So far, you have been fired nine times. Which is a lot. For anyone. Sometimes it will be sucky, but other times it will be quite joyful. There is always unemployment, and who doesn't need a job sabbatical? Put aside the cursing oils and spells, because if there's one person who can do her job exquisitely well, it's karma. To date, every single person who has ever fired you has subsequently lost his or her job, too, except for two of them. But there is still time. There is still time. Heh heh heh.

If people in your life are important to you, let them know. And not just when you're drunk. In fact, never when you're drunk. The only thing you get to do when you're drunk is laugh, otherwise you might end up on a picnic table in a park somewhere, and that is gross and whorey, Alicia. What I mean is never hesitate to tell a friend how much you miss them if you haven't seen them for a while. If you think someone is awesome, make sure they know. Do nice things for people when you get an opportunity to without going overboard. Maybe I'm sentimental now, but I'm old enough to know that the most important thing in your life is the people around you. Nothing else means shit. Hug Nana when she's not expecting it. Dance with Pop Pop when he puts on Bobby Darin and asks you. You might try telling Mom that you love her. (Spoiler alert: In 2016, she might say it back.)

The day that you cut all the green stuff off of the moz-

zarella in the fridge and use the rest for eggplant Parme-
san because you don't want to go to the store—go to the
store. The mere flicker of the thought of it creates tsuna-
mis of nausea that will haunt you for years and years and
years to come.

And finally—

On second thought, do talk to the guy who looks like
Gregg Allman at the party. Do talk to him. Do watch him
bang his head against a fence, and do stand there while he
drives away without you. Because of him, you will miss
your macroeconomics exam, that's true, but more important, you will tell this story to the nicest guy you know.
He's also the cutest boy you know. Well, he's the one. I
know you think he's out of your league, and he is, but *he*
doesn't know that. And when you get married, and he
says that he wants to wear a shalwar kameez, you should
probably let him. 'Cause the window is gonna close on
that pretty soon.

I'll see you sooner than you think.

Awesomely,

Laurie

ACKNOWLEDGMENTS

A bottomless well of gratitude to Pamela Cannon and Libby Maguire for everything; to Beth Pearson, Amelia Zalcman, Joe Perez, and Betsy Wilson for their vital and valued contributions; to my family, especially my nephew Nick, who lets me embarrass him in public again and again; to my neighbors, for tolerating our inability to bring our trash and recycling bins back in on time; to my husband, for being the funniest guy I know; to my dog, Maeby, for being the cute little pig she is; and always, and entirely, to Jenny Bent.

Thank you Amy Silverman, Amy Segal, Claire Lawton, Cindy Dach, Lore Carillo, Laura Greenberg, Meg Halverson, Louise Bishop, David Dunton, Robrt Pela, Jeff Abbott, Colleen Steinberg, Bruce Tracy, Nina Graybill, Nancy Ragghianti, Angela Lindig, Michelle Jennings, Michelle Loyet, Chrissy Porter, Kim Veilleux, Teri Queen, and Jacob Barto, and my friends, early readers, and chorus.

But most of all, thank you to you, for reading this far. Writers without readers are just lonely people at keyboards. I can't do what I do without you, and I truly, deeply, madly appreciate it. I mean it.

Xoxoxox,

Laurie

LAURIE NOTARO is the *New York Times*
bestselling author of ten books, misses her
Nana, and loves to read in bed. She lives
in Eugene, Oregon, where she sees many
women each day in dire need of foundations
(the undergarments, not the charities,
although they could probably use those,
too). She has a husband (still) and a dog,
Maeby, whom she has taught to play
hide-and-seek.